Can Modern War Be Just?

Can Modern War Be Just?

JAMES TURNER JOHNSON

Yale University Press
New Haven and London

Published with assistance from
the Louis Stern Memorial Fund.

Designed by James J. Johnson
and set in Aster Roman type.
Printed in the United States of America by
Murray Printing Company, Westford, Mass.

*The paper in this book meets the guidelines for
permanence and durability of the Committee on
Production Guidelines for Book Longevity of the
Council on Library Resources.*

Library of Congress Cataloging in Publication Data

Johnson, James Turner.
  Can modern war be just?

  Bibliography: p.
  Includes index.
  1. War—Moral and ethical aspects. 2. Just war
doctrine. I. Title.
U21.2.J627   1984   172'.42   84–3523
ISBN 0–300–03165–3

10 9 8 7 6 5 4 3 2 1

Contents

that may be morally employed in case of need; the implications of
this thesis for weapons research and development and for the
question of the military draft.

Preface

This book has its origins in a number of lectures I have given and essays I have written over the past several years as contributions to the contemporary debate on morality and warfare. As one who has analyzed the growth and development of the major Western moral tradition on war—the "just war" tradition—I have often been challenged with the assertion that this tradition has no meaning in the current debate; this book is in part a response to those challenges. But more directly and more positively, it is the result of being invited to explore the contemporary meaning of just war tradition in a number of recent conferences, journals, and collections of essays.

The debate over morality and war in this country has a way of heating up and cooling down, then beginning again. Each new cycle in some ways repeats the old, while adding different dimensions reflecting changes in the political environment, weapons systems, current strategic and tactical theory and practice, and sometimes in the nature of moral awareness. The chapters in this book clearly reflect the cycle of debate over nuclear strategy and national defense that began in the last years of the Carter administration and turned sharply upward in the first years of the Reagan presidency. Because my arguments have been focused by the particulars of this stage in the debate, some of the specific matters treated—for example, the cruise missile and the neutron warhead, "decapitation" strategy, the return to favor of conventional weaponry, and thought about "war-fighting" capabilities—may very well be as archaic to discuss after a few years as the argument over deployment of the "atomic cannon" sounds to us now. But the moral issues before us today are substantially the same as those raised in earlier cycles of the debate, and in the context of this book these specific contemporary examples of weaponry and strategic and tactical thought serve chiefly as focal points around which to develop the implications of the moral tradition of just war. The book may thus be read on two levels: as a contribution to the immediate debate, conditioned by concern over how morally to reach a judgment on specific matters such as the ones mentioned, or as a contribution to moral analysis and understanding of just war tradition, here approached as a guide to practical moral decisions and not, as in my other books, through its historical development.

The intent throughout, in any case, is to bring just war perspectives to bear on the problems posed by contemporary ways of thinking about war and means of force available to employ in case of war. Though there is much written below on current weaponry, and particularly on nuclear weapons, I am convinced that these are more symptoms than causes of the moral problem of war today. More fundamental is how we think of the place of force in political life and how we conceive the ability of contemporary nations to employ the means of force available to them in ways compatible with human values. If just war thinking is, to its critics, irrelevant to contemporary war, that is because they have lost sight of the possibility that, in some circumstances, force may be all that remains to protect and preserve values, and because they have passed negative judgment on present human capabilities to control and limit the force available to nations so as to keep it subservient to higher values and principles.

I have benefited a great deal in preparing this book from conferences, symposia, and private discussions in which I have been involved during the past several years. These include a symposium at the Woodrow Wilson Center for Scholars in Washington, D.C., held in October 1978, where I read an early version of a paper that eventually developed into chapter 2 of this book; the annual meeting of the Society of Christian Ethics held in New York during January 1980, where the paper that became chapter 4 was presented; and a conference of the Institute for Theological Encounter with Science and Technology in St. Louis during October 1981, where I read what later became chapter 3. Apart from these occasions from which specific chapters have sprung I would mention several others, which have influenced my thinking no less strongly if more generally: an invitation to deliver the D. R. Sharpe Memorial Lecture at the University of Chicago Divinity School in April 1982; in the same month, a symposium organized by the American Society of Church History, meeting in Richmond, Virginia, at which I was asked to read a paper; an invitation to lecture at the U.S. Army Major Command Chaplains' Conference in July 1982; another invitation to give a paper and participate in discussions at a conference hosted by Concordia College, Moorhead, Minnesota, in September 1982, and sponsored by the college and the Minnesota Committee for the Humanities; and a request to read a paper at the Conference on Faith and History of the American Historical Association, meeting in Washington in December 1982. At this point the first draft of the book was complete, but final revisions made during the summer of 1983 benefited as well from further discussions made possible by several other invitations to lecture: at a symposium for bishops of the Lutheran Church in America, Washington, March 1983; at a conference on the American Catholic bishops' pastoral letter held at Duquesne University that same month; at a conference of Duodecim held in Washington the following month; and at the United States Military Academy's Senior Conference XXI, held at West Point in June 1983. Over the last several years I have frequently been asked to lecture in the weekend seminars of the Georgetown University Program in National Security Studies; one such occasion was in March 1983.

There are too many individuals from whom I have

learned—civilian and military, academics in various fields, professional strategists, and others—for me to name them all here, though they clearly include the people with whom I have talked during the occasions mentioned above. I need also, though, to mention in particular the lengthy conversations I have had on a number of occasions with Chaplain (Major) Donald Davidson, United States Army, currently a member of the faculty at the Army War College, Carlisle Barracks, Pennsylvania, and with Professor William V. O'Brien of the department of government, Georgetown University.

Mrs. Brigid M. Brown not only typed the manuscript (in several stages, in the case of some chapters) but regularly engaged me in discussions about the book that helped me to clarify my thoughts and language in many instances.

A final note on how to read this book may be useful. The normal way, of course, is to begin at the beginning and read through to the end. For the reader who goes from first to last, the attempt is to provide a comprehensive overview of major areas of moral concern posed by contemporary war as these appear in just war perspective. But this normal way of reading may not be the most usual way. As already mentioned, many of the chapters below have their antecedents in discrete papers prepared for specific occasions. I have attempted to retain that discrete character in preparing this book, so that it will be possible for a person interested in only one or another issue at a given time to read only the chapter or chapters related to it. In my experience, this is how such a book as this is in practice often used, especially by students. Such a method of writing, though, tends to produce some redundancies, since the same thematic issues arise in different sets of contexts. I have tried to minimize such overlap, but where it occurs cross-references are given so that the issues under discussion can be followed in all the contexts. These cross-references should also facilitate chapter-by-chapter "dipping in," where that is the reading method followed. The notes and bibliography are intended not only to locate my own thinking within contemporary discussion but also to guide further exploration by readers interested in pursuing further the nature of just war tradition and its implications for moral debate over the place of force in the politics of nations.

I conclude by thanking my wife, Pamela, for her encouragement of my efforts and for making easier the time I have spent writing, and my children, Christopher and Ashley, for their tolerant acceptance of their father's often time-consuming involvement in the debate over morality and contemporary war. The book is dedicated to Chris and Ashley, and to others of their generation, who will next have to shoulder the burdens of moral life and political responsibility.

Can Modern War Be Just?

Introduction
The Restraint of War in
Western Moral Tradition

During the first part of the fifth century of the Christian era, Augustine of Hippo, revered today as a saint in the Catholic faith and yet also deeply influential on Protestant theology, set down in writing certain ideas on the use of violence that have had a decisive impact on thought about war in Western culture. Augustine wrote as a Christian theologian, dealing with a problem that clearly for him was profoundly painful: how to reconcile traditional Christian teaching against the use of violence with the need to defend the Roman Empire—Christian for more than a century by Augustine's time—from the invading Vandals. The solution he reached—a justification of war under certain prescribed circumstances, yet with genuine limits on the harm that could be done even in a justified war—is generally regarded as the beginning of just war doctrine in Christian teaching, as well as a major contribution to the development of consensual Western thought on the restraint of war.

That there exists a consensual tradition in Western culture on the justification and limitation of war will be a surprise to persons who think of war as inherently incapable of restraint and of justifying reasons for war as being convenient rationalizations of state power. Yet every culture has some such tradition, and ours has remained remarkably consistent (though going through considerable development) right up into the contemporary period, where it finds expression in international law, in military manuals of the laws and customs of war, in moral debate over nuclear arms and strategic doctrines like Mutual Assured Destruction, in the concept of conscientious objection to military service. In a fundamental sense we in the West cannot think about war without using the terms of this broad tradition, even if we disagree with what it teaches. And for this reason if for no other, it is important to understand what is implied by this dual theme of permission to engage in violence accompanied by clearly enunciated restraints on that violence. For my own part, I would have us understand this tradition for another, perhaps more pressing, reason: the experience of all-out war in the two global conflicts of this century has led a great many people to think that the use of military force must inevitably be total and unrestrained, and the problem is not simply that by thinking this way we are being unfaithful to our roots. Rather, given the destructive power of modern weaponry, to conceive of the use of force in this totalistic, unlimited way is to put the world in enormous danger. Having largely forgotten the lessons on the good of restraint in war discovered when weapons themselves imposed some limits, we have the greater responsibility to recover those lessons in a time when the only restraints on the destructiveness of war can be those set by purposeful human choice.

It is suggestive to begin our recovery with Augustine on defense. Taken as a model, this case has the disadvantage of saying little on the question of when resort to force is justified between nations, but it has the overwhelming advantage of pointing in the direction taken by subsequent efforts to define limits on the use of force. As this is the problem on which most contemporary debate focuses, in this book I concentrate on it. In classic terminology the whole range of issues on the management of force is covered by the phrase *jus in bello*, meaning literally what it is right or just to do in war, while the issues pertaining to whether to resort to war are collectively grouped under the heading *jus ad bellum*.

Our focus thus will be on the *jus in bello* of the just war tradition, the broad cultural consensus on appropriate limits to force that has developed over Western history. (The *jus in bello*, as we shall see in more detail below, proceeds from two fundamental ideas: the need to protect noncombatants in wartime and the need for the means of war to be proportionate to the tasks of war. The *jus ad bellum* includes such concepts as just cause, right authority, right intention, that the resort to war be a last resort, and proportionality in a larger, overall sense weighing the total evil a war would cause against whatever good it can be expected to achieve. In this connection, a further idea is generally added as part of the *just ad bellum* criteria: that the goal of a war be peace, or at least a more secure peace than that which obtained beforehand. Such, at least, is the *jus ad bellum* in *moral* terms. In contemporary international law these ideas tend to be collapsed into regulations defining aggression and the proper limits of defense.)

Augustine treated defense by means of a paradigmatic situation involving three persons: a criminal who is attacking or about to attack a second person, the innocent victim, and a third person, an onlooker, on whose behalf Augustine offers his thoughts. What should this third person do in such a situation? We must recall that Augustine wrote within a Christian context in which the use of violence had been generally deplored: in telling his disciple Peter to sheath his sword, so the argument went, Jesus had in principle disarmed all Christians. But Augustine was not convinced by this, and his argument advanced toward a quite different conclusion. The onlooker, as Christian, must be motivated by love toward both those individuals before him, the criminal as well as the victim. Yet the criminal, who is armed, is unjustly aggressing against the innocent weaponless victim. The proper action for the Christian, reasoned Augustine, is to intervene between criminal and victim, defending the latter even at the risk of his own life against attack or threat of attack by the former. Such defense of the victim, argued Augustine, is mandated by the onlooker's love for him as someone for whom Christ died; yet Christ also died for the criminal, and this limits what may be done toward him in defending the innocent victim. Briefly stated, Augustine argued for a proportionate response to the threat represented by the criminal: the onlooker should seek to prevent the criminal from carrying out his evil intention by defensive measures designed to thwart whatever the criminal may try. Escalation here is made the attacker's responsibility, not the defender's. The latter may meet force with proportionately effective force right up to and including the possibility of killing the criminal, if he does not relent before that. Meanwhile, the Christian onlooker, now become his innocent neighbor's defender, is not in any sense guilty for doing what he must, for he is acting the only way he can when motivated by love: opposing the doing of evil, yet separating his hatred for evil from his love for the person of the evildoer.

Though couched in centrally Christian terminology and forms of thought, Augustine's argument here introduces in sharp definition the two moral principles that have historically defined the *jus in bello:* the ideas of proportionality and discrimination or noncombatant immunity. Augustine's criminal stands for any soldier who menaces an unarmed noncombatant peacefully going about his business. Transferred to the context of war, the criminal and the defender who opposes him become enemy soldiers on the battlefield, and the purpose of war is defined in terms of the defense of peaceful life and resistance to evil actions. But opposition to the enemy's evil should not imply hatred for the enemy soldiers. Augustine's reason for this was a theological one: Christ died for the evildoers as well as for the just. But in its later development this idea was radically secularized into what is known today as the principle of humanity. Its meaning was well stated by the eighteenth-century Swiss theorist of international law, Emmerich de Vattel: "Let us never forget," he wrote, "that our enemies are men." Augustine could not have put this idea more pungently. The principle of humanity underlies the modern law of war, providing its own moral underpinning to the ideas of proportion and noncombatant immunity, though these concepts are rooted as well in the idea of justice. From their roots in Christian theorizing about violence, then, the essential concepts of restraint in war have over the centuries become secularized, and the values undergirding them have ceased to be specifically those of Christian religion but have become perceived as generic to Western culture.

This transformation began in the Middle Ages, ironically that time in Western history when Christian religion and secular life were most closely intertwined. We can identify four distinct streams that fed into the coalescing consensus on war during this period. Two were specifically Christian: the input of scholastic theology and the related, though separate and distinctive, input of the canon lawyers. The other two streams of influence are based in traditions outside those preserved by the church: one from the civil law, based principally in Roman theory and practice, and one from the realm of chivalric life, based in both an indigenous class tradition and in considerations of realpolitik. The chivalric input into the developing idea of noncombatant immunity—or more accurately, the reasons behind the development of a uniquely chivalric idea of noncombatant immunity—will illustrate how secular forces have shaped and transformed just war tradition. Stated succinctly, it appears that knights had two important reasons for guaranteeing the protection of noncombatants. First, there was no glory in armed combat with a nonknight, for knights were professionals. Indeed, killing nonknights would create a bad reputation, not a good one. Second, noncombatant serfs, peasants, artisans, and merchants were the source of the wealth of members of the knightly class. Besides it being cowardly to attack an enemy through his noncombatant subjects rather than directly, each propertied member of the chivalric class had a positive interest in protecting the lives and livelihoods of the noncombatants who supported him. Both considerations gave chivalry, quite apart from specifically Christian influence, its own doctrine of noncombatant immunity, and this became joined to the other streams mentioned above in a generalized cultural consensus by the close of the Middle Ages.

This point can be generalized for the history of the development of the tradition as a whole. To take another outstanding example, much of the modern law of war, as well as contemporary doctrines of limited war, derives from the practice of "sovereigns' war" during the eighteenth century, including the wars of Frederick the Great of Prussia against virtually all of his neighboring monarchs and the wars collectively known in American history as the WAG wars (King William's, Queen Anne's, King George's wars). These were conflicts among monarchs and their private armies, not, as became the practice after the French Revolution, wars involving entire populations of one state against another. In this foremost example of limited warfare in Western history the restraint was largely due to necessity and what was perceived as necessity, not to conscious reflection on the moral tradition of restraint in war. Yet contributions to moral traditions do not themselves have to go by the name of *moral* ideas or practices, as morality is narrowly conceived. Thus the practices of restraint regularized in the sovereigns' wars have become a recognizable and significant part of the developing tradition, illustrating how, for example, considerations of military necessity can sometimes be joined to those of humanity to mitigate the cruelty of war.

The final transformation of the value base of the just war tradition away from the specifically Christian was accomplished at the dawn of the modern period, beginning with the work of a Spanish Dominican, Franciscus de Victoria, and completed by the time of the jurists Alberico Gentili and Hugo Grotius. The men who effected this transformation are the collective fathers of modern international law, and international law has been one of the major vehicles through which the tradition of restraint in war has been maintained and further developed in the modern period. But to speak of a transformation to a secular value base for the tradition means only that now these ideas of restraint are clearly the property of Western culture—and by extension through international law, world culture—rather than narrowly the values of any specific religious faith. This in turn implies that while certainly debate on morality and war may go on within Christian theological ethics or the ethics of any other religion, debate in the public sphere should be in terms of the values of the larger society. The best contribution by theologians might be to uncover persuasively for all to see whatever it is that is unique in their own transcendence-based analysis of morality in war. In this way they contribute to the public life of the nation and the world, rather than only to the life of their own religious community.

Unfortunately, though, it is by no means clear that moral analysts, whether theological or not, have done their best in examining the implications of the traditional *jus in bello* ideas for contemporary warfare. For example, countercity targeting of strategic nuclear warheads flies directly in the face of the idea of noncombatant immunity, and terrorism also directly challenges the right of peaceful noncombatants to live their lives in safety. The deep erosion of the idea that noncombatants should be spared may be seen in the degree of support received by Lieutenant Calley in the My Lai case, in spite of the prohibition of such acts as his in military regulations, international law on war, and just war tradition broadly speaking. To recover for contemporary issues the moral wisdom developed in just war tradition thus is a matter of some importance, and this defines the scope of the following chapters.

Is it possible to identify, before we turn to the arguments in detail, what sorts of implications for contemporary war ought to be drawn from just war tradition? For my part, I am convinced that the tradition unambiguously points in the direction of counterforce rather than counterpopulation targeting of strategic weapons, toward the development of weapons that are inherently capable of being used more discriminatingly and proportionately in war than those currently available, and toward enhanced conventional warfare capabilities. While any kind of nuclear war might well be destructive out of proportion to almost any conceivable value it might serve, there is ample evidence that counterforce targeting is at least a part of both American and Soviet strategic planning, and this represents a step in the right direction, by contrast to the era of massive retaliation in the

1950s. Consideration of the rights of noncombatants demands no less than this and implies that we should try to do more. So far as new weapons are concerned, considerations of both proportionality and discrimination point toward such developments as laser weaponry to replace blast and radiation weapons, as well as space warfare capability to remove the likely theater of battle as far as possible from the populations inhabiting the surface of the earth. (These last implications, clearly, have chiefly to do with research and development.) Closer to hand, both proportionality and discrimination support the replacement of tactical fission warheads with low-yield fusion weapons. Further, this line of moral reasoning implies the enhancement of conventional warfare capabilities, not because contemporary conventional warfare is not destructive but because it is less destructive and its effects more controllable than nuclear war. Because nuclear weapons are undoubtedly a great deal cheaper than an equivalent conventional force, replacing draftees with missiles has been politically popular. For these reasons the nuclear arms race has been fueled by the trend away from conventional forces. So far as nuclear armaments represent the denial of restraint in war, concern to impose restraint on any possible use of military force in the future suggests a reversing of direction, even at economic and political cost, toward more and better conventional forces.

Such practical suggestions as these may be debated, but debate over practical matters is the very meat and bones of Western tradition on the restraint of war. This has not been a moral tradition formulated and preserved in a vacuum, and recovery of just war tradition would seem to imply not only efforts of historical and moral analysis aimed at clarifying past developments in the tradition, but also—and perhaps more important—the creation of a public debate aimed at applying this bit of our cultural wisdom to contemporary realities. The following chapters are offered in this spirit.

I

The Context

1

The Utility of Just War Categories for Moral Analysis of Contemporary War

It is difficult to think in just war terms about contemporary international affairs, including war as an aspect of the possible relations among nations, because of certain misconceptions about what is meant by thinking "in just war terms." This chapter is partly concerned with identifying and correcting some of the most important misconceptions. Still, if this were the only problem confronting us in attempting to reflect morally on war, we would have an easier task than we do: we might simply scrap the traditional categories, terminology, and ideals and start from scratch to invent new ones to fit the case immediately before us. Whether this would, in fact, be an easier course is not at all clear, but in any case it is not open to us. The name *just war* stands for a broadly and consensually shaped moral tradition in Western culture on the problems of justifying and restraining the violence of war; as products of that culture, we cannot shuck off these traditional ways of thinking by a simple act of will. If one side of the dilemma before us is how to apply the moral wisdom contained in just war tradition to the case of contemporary war, the other side is that we cannot escape doing so.[1] Thus we must confront our misconceptions in order to cope with this dilemma, for only in clarifying the nature of this moral tradition and its relation to our own identity as moral agents shaped by a powerful cultural heritage can we resolve the problems posed in this dilemmatic way.

Two kinds of misconceptions need to be set right: those about the nature of just war tradition as a whole and those about individual features or moral categories defined within the tradition. I will begin with the former, since much of the argument in the preceding paragraph depends on what the tradition as a whole is conceived to be.

What Is Just War Tradition?

What is before us is not a *doctrine*, as it is often called, especially in religious circles, but a *tradition* including many individual doctrines from various sources within the culture and various periods of historical development and representing variations in content. If we would speak of "just war doctrine," we are immediately confronted by a bewildering multiplicity. We must ask, "Whose doctrine?" and end up favoring one or the other lifted up out of the whole. This approach often results in historical positivism about morals: so-and-so said this is what to think or do, so that's what I must think or do. A Catholic who depends too heavily on the (comparatively minimal) just war theory of Thomas Aquinas would provide one example of this wrong way of thinking about just war tradition as a single doctrine; other examples would include Protestants who overuse Augustine, Luther, or even the Bible in this way and international lawyers who attempt to lift the modern law of war as a unit out of its historical context. By contrast with such approaches, thinking of just war tradition requires entering the circle of continuing development of that tradition, regarding each of its various historical contributors as coparticipants worthy to be heard and necessary to be taken seriously, but not as prophets to be followed blindly. Just war tradition as a guide to moral analysis requires active moral judgment within a historical context that includes not only the contemporary world but the significantly remembered past. It cannot properly be a basis for historical positivism in ethics.

Another widespread misconception is to think of just war ideas as being the more or less exclusive property of Christian—and more specifically, Catholic—moral thought. On this view the just war tradition is first and foremost a product of specifically theological wisdom and a repository of narrowly Christian ethical principles having some bearing on relations among states. There are several things wrong with this way of conceiving the nature of just war tradition. Admittedly, Christian theologians have had an important impact on the development of this historical moral tradition; otherwise it would not represent, as I have asserted above, a culture-wide moral consensus on the justification and limitation of war. But in the first place, these specifically Christian contributions have not come only or even principally from the theologians; canon law and the traditions of the confessional, both sources closer to the dirtiness and moral ambiguity of ordinary life than is theology as a discipline of thought, have contributed as much or more fundamentally to shaping the peculiarly Christian inputs into the developing historical tradition on just war. Indeed, in the twelfth and thirteenth centuries, when the just war tradition as a coherent body of ideas and practices began to coalesce, it was not the theologians but the canonists within the European ecclesiastical establishment who dealt most forcefully, sustainedly, and thoroughly with matters of morality relating to warfare.[2] Second, the Christian contributors are not properly thought of as Catholics in the modern denominational sense. There was no Catholic Church, in this sense, before the events of the Reformation and the Counter-Reformation. Earlier there is only Christendom, the common heritage of modern Protestants and Catholics alike, and, because of the commonality of Christian faith in the West in this era, the heritage as well of modern secular culture. Again, what we confront in just war tradition is a multifaceted and various unity of moral insights and practices reflecting the experience and judgments of historical persons across the whole breadth of cultural institutions. The relegation of just war ideas to a narrow sphere of peculiarly Christian (or Catholic, in the modern sense) theological reflection is wrong not only because it is bad history, but because it incorrectly attempts to separate our own identity from a portion of our common cultural past.

One of the most astonishing aspects of the historical development of just war tradition is how much it owes to secular sources, some of them, like the military, thought by many people not to have anything to do with morality at all. This is a poor understanding of morality which relegates it to the cloisters of ecclesiastical life. In fact the historical origin and much of the early development of the ideas defining the limits of permissible violence in war was in the military sphere.[3] Medieval Christianity produced a *jus ad bellum*, but the *jus in bello* came out of the customs and sensibilities of the knightly class, who provided the professional soldiers of their time. Similarly it is necessary to credit later *jus in bello* developments importantly to the early modern manuals of military conduct, such as Gustavus Adolphus's *Swedish Discipline* in the Thirty Years War, to later military practice like that of the sovereigns' wars of the eighteenth century, still later to developments within military professional self-consciousness like the Union Army's *General Orders No. 100* in the American Civil War and, finally, to the contemporary discussion on professionalism within the United States military. All of these are the subject of a chapter below; at this point what is necessary is to note that they properly belong to the continuing historical development of just war tradition, right alongside its other component parts, including Christian religion and secular law.

I have already alluded in passing to the mistaken conception that Western moral tradition on war can be reduced to what is contained in international law on war. Modern international law is one of the bearers of this tradition—one among others. It is, moreover, a continuation of the line of effort begun by nonecclesiastical lawyers in the Middle Ages who were concerned to identify the implications of the natural law and the "law of nations," as they conceived these in the terminology of classical Rome, to the conduct of war in their day. Modern international law as a discrete discipline of thought rose out of the broader consensual just war tradition at the birth of the modern era by means of the combined work of neo-scholastic theologians like Franciscus de Victoria and Francisco Suarez and early publicists like Alberico Gentili and Hugo Grotius. But even as this discipline of thought arose, it defined its own parameters, thereby ruling out some kinds of concerns while including and magnifying others. Thus it is a misconception to think of the international law of war as it has developed down to our own time as containing all that there is to say about the justification and limitation of war. At least two other major lines of development have to be laid alongside it for the outlines of the whole to emerge: military professionalism in theory and practice, as noted above, and moral concerns both secular and religious, newly defined in the modern period as distinguishable disciplines of thought by themselves.

Implicit in all that I have been saying thus far is a rejection of yet another wrong conception: that just war tradition has only to do with ideas and thus is abstractedly remote from real-life circumstances, which require not ideas but actions. This is far from the truth. Just war tradition represents above all a fund of *practical* moral wisdom, based not in abstract speculation or theorization but in reflection on actual problems encountered in war as these have presented themselves in different historical circumstances. Thus, for example, I have taken pains to note that military *practice* has functioned in the development and bearing of the tradition. Indeed, without such a fundamental rooting in practical concerns, it is hard to see what would be the point of asking about the meaning of just war tradition in the context of contemporary war. While I, like other writers, often use terms like "moral thought" and "ideas," they function as a kind of shorthand to indicate the practice and product of reflection on practical realities. As I have argued above, thinking about war in terms of just war tradition means allowing one's own individual reflections to be guided by the experience and reflections of others in a rich cultural history who have attempted to deal with practical problems both similar and dissimilar to our own. This requires that we look at the practices of war as well as at moral theorizing about war to "keep faith" with this tradition.

Still, though, it is necessary to hold that critical and constructive moral thought provides an indispensable balance to the purely practical side of just war tradition. Only the theorist can take the long view; only the theorist can analyze, summarize, cut through deadwood, identify wrong turns, and draw out the implications of positive elements in the developing tradition. The need for moral theoretical input into the process of development was substantially forgotten through much of the nineteenth century, and I believe this is one reason why in world wars I and II Western culture came to accept the rightness of unlimited means of war—the shelling of cities and gas warfare in World War I, and in World War II the obliteration of population centers by conventional explosives, napalm, and finally by atomic weapons. That our culture has come to accept such an intentionality as this concept of "total war" is directly counter to the meaning of the entire tradition that treats warfare as sometimes justifiable, yet always to be practiced within limits, with restraint. A significant portion of the role of the contemporary moral theorist dealing with war is to remind the larger culture that, in terms of its own highest values as they have taken shape and been expressed over history, the turn toward total war has been a wrong turn: war does not have to be total; it is possible to think again, as in the past, of justified force that may be employed with restraint.

The Question of Adequacy

When we ask about the adequacy of any system of moral guidance, we are in fact asking three separate but related questions:

1. Is the system "right"? That is, does it correspond to the moral values of the culture or community in which it has come into existence and in which the identity of the moral agent has been shaped?
2. Does this system provide an adequate conceptual framework for moral analysis and judgment?
3. Does this system represent a bridging of the gap between the ideal and the possible? That is, does it produce practical moral

guidance as well as identify the relevant moral values for the situation at hand?

To sustain the claims I have been making about the real nature of just war tradition and its central place in Western moral reflection on war would be to answer all three of these questions positively. Indeed, it would be to say more: only through examination of just war tradition do we discover who we are and what are our moral values relative to war and violence. So the question of correspondence turns out to be a two-way street. As to whether the conceptual framework is adequate, we must seriously ask what else might replace such concepts as justice, proportionality, the need to protect non-combatants, the requirement that force be a last resort, and so on. There may be other concepts that are more adequate, but that is like saying that there may be life in the fifth dimension; we simply cannot know because our knowledge is limited by the circumstances of our existence. People in our culture cannot escape thinking about morality and war in terms like these, and this is the reason why just war tradition has come together as it has. This is, of course, not at all the same as saying that conclusions reached everywhere and at all times must be identical, and indeed the diversity within the tradition itself should warn us away from such a claim. But it is to affirm that we begin with a generally common set of moral perceptions and share a common language of moral discourse. And this is quite a lot. Finally, as to the question of practical moral guidance, in the present context I will only recall that the theoretical and the practical have intermingled at every stage in the historical development of this tradition. The world of just war ideas is the world of practical realities in the relations among states; yet at the same time the moral values defined here represent a window on the ideal. Together these produce a system of moral guidance capable of judging whether a particular decision to employ force is justified or not, whether a particular level or type of force used is right or wrong. This is nothing less than what is meant by practical moral guidance.

Of course, at this point to say all this about the adequacy

of just war tradition as a system of moral guidance is to make yet another claim. The relation most of us in the contemporary world have to this tradition of moral reflection is analogous to the situation of the person who was greatly surprised to discover that he had been speaking prose all his life. Most of us have not consciously recognized how we think about war and violence or even tried consciously to be consistent in identifying or applying moral judgments to the realities before us. One of the chief purposes of this book is to help to improve such moral consciousness and consistency, and the place of the present chapter within this whole is to make clear what claims are implied by this and to provide a general overview of what it means to think consciously in the manner defined in just war tradition. Each of the following chapters has its own place within this larger aim, but the problem before us here is to begin to come to terms with what just war tradition is as a unity. Certain general misconceptions have already been identified; now it is time to turn to several particular components of the tradition, some of the major ideas around which the tradition has coalesced, to attempt to establish what meaning they in fact have within this tradition and, proleptically, how their meaning should be understood now.

Major Just War Concepts

In the classic terminology, the component parts of just war theory are grouped under two headings, as follows:

jus ad bellum	*jus in bello*
(whether resort to force is justified)	(whether a particular form of the use of force is justified)
just cause	
right authority	proportionality (in the sense of proximate good over evil)
right intent	
proportionality (in the sense of total good and evil anticipated)	discrimination, or noncombatant protection
the end of peace	
last resort	

The *jus ad bellum* is, in other words, that portion of the tradition that deals with the justification of force, while the *jus in bello* addresses restraints or limits on how force may be used. The latter is sometimes defined as having to do with weapons limitation and noncombatant protection; yet weapons limits have to do with both moral principles, proportionality and discrimination. With this in mind, one can use either terminology depending on context, and both ways of speaking about the restraint of force are employed in this book.

In the following discussion I wish to comment briefly on five ideas, three from the first column, one from the second, and one found under both rubrics, addressing pertinent misconceptions, attempting to establish what content the tradition has given to each idea, and asking what relevance these notions have to contemporary issues.

1. The requirement that every use of force be in a *just cause* is possibly the most inclusive idea within just war tradition. Historically at least four separate and somewhat different contents have been assigned to it. In Augustine's discussion of the defense of the neighbor an *interventionist* conception of just cause was at work: it is the Christian's duty, reasoned Augustine (and, by extension, the duty of any just state), to intervene on behalf of innocent neighbors who are the object of aggression.[4] Thomas Aquinas expanded this concept[5] by reflection on a Pauline passage (Romans 13:4) referring to the duties of those who rule: "[The prince] is minister of God, to come in wrath to punish evildoers." On this conception the principal justifying cause for use of force is the need for *punishment.* Third, there is the notion that *defense* always constitutes a just cause. This idea is as old as the ages and is, at least in theory, the only legitimating cause for resort to war allowed in contemporary international law. I will return to this concept of just cause below. Finally, there is the conception that all "holy" wars are just, which has its secular counterpart in the various concepts of ideological war, "war of national liberation," "peoples' war," war for "supreme emergency," and so on. This is really a limiting case of the just cause idea, and it differs

from the other three causes mentioned in legitimating unrestrained use of force. Ironically, a persistent theme in American attitudes in this century has been that only this extreme kind of cause is worth taking seriously, and only all-out warfare is worth fighting.[6] The self-righteousness implicit in this conception of just cause is, however, difficult if not impossible to justify, and the weight of just war tradition accordingly points the other way, toward justifying only limited uses of force for limited causes.

All these conceptions are, of course, rooted in the idea of fault: for a just cause to exist, the purpose of war must be to redress in some way a wrong done by the enemy. But in the real world fault is not always unilateral or easy to assign, and this raises problems with the idea that there must be a just cause for war. The first questions were raised as early as the fourteenth century, during the Hundred Years War between the French and English monarchs and their forces. According to English law, which allowed accession to a throne through a female relative, the English king rightly should have sat on the throne of France. But according to French law, which recognized descent through the male line only, the English claim was invalid. To further complicate the situation, the English monarch was also titular lord of several holdings that made him, according to feudal custom, a vassal of the French king. Yet the two kings, as reigning monarchs, were also formally equals. In such a complex situation, where did just cause lie? Though the question could be posed, the solution was not reached in the medieval context. Only in the sixteenth and seventeenth centuries, in the writings of Victoria and Grotius, did a way out of this perplexity become apparent.[7]

Considering the case of the Indians of the New World and whether they had a right to defend themselves against the Spanish explorers and missionaries, Victoria invoked the concept of invincible ignorance. In war, he argued, one side may *be* in the right, while the other, by invincible ignorance, may *believe* itself in the right. Indeed, it is possible to conceive of wars in which both belligerents are deceived by such ignorance into thinking that they each have a just cause, when in fact neither does. In such cases the question is not of objective versus subjective just causes, because even an objective third-party observer may be unable to disentangle conflicting claims so as to adjudicate the matter. So, Victoria concludes, in such cases both sides should be treated as if they had just cause, and both sides must consider themselves scrupulously bound by the limits of the *jus in bello*, the law of war.

The *jus ad bellum*, here focused closely on the element of just cause, was thus resolved by Victoria into a doctrine of simultaneous ostensible justice. Grotius followed Victoria in this, taking the further step of diluting the moral purpose of the *jus ad bellum* by emphasizing its formal side, the need for both belligerents to declare their intents and claims publicly for all to see and judge. The result was to undercut the *jus ad bellum* for nearly three centuries but at the same time to give more weight to the moral and legal efforts aimed at managing force in war, the *jus in bello*.

In the twentieth century international law has attempted to recover the notion of just cause in war, thereby attempting to reassert the importance of the considerations known in the historical tradition by the name of *jus ad bellum*. Beginning with the League of Nations Covenant and the Pact of Paris (or Kellogg-Briand Pact), and continuing in articles 2 and 51 of the United Nations Charter, the effort has been to outlaw aggressive war while accepting defense as a legitimate cause for going to war.[8] While surely it is a good thing for there to be some legal recognition of the moral principle that there needs to be a justifying cause for waging war, there is nonetheless a serious question, from the point of view of moral analysis, whether this particular way of treating the matter is not too reductionistic. In the first place, the same sort of ambiguity that surfaced in the Hundred Years War and between the Spanish explorers and the Indians appears here as well. Consider the problem of how to define aggression: is the aggressor the one who fires the first shot, or are there other kinds of aggression that are perhaps more important? In the 1967 Arab–Israeli war President de Gaulle of France used the former criterion as the basis for denouncing the preemptive attack by Israeli forces; yet Israel argued here that the genuine aggression was in the acts of the Arab nations in the period before the outbreak of fighting: specifically, the latter were issuing statements calling for the annihilation of Israel, had closed the Straits of Tiran to Israeli ships, had joined in mutual support agreements, and had assembled their military forces in apparent preparation for a coordinated attack. The attempt to render just cause in the contemporary terms of an aggressor–defender dichotomy does not escape the ambiguity that, in an earlier age, led to the concept of simultaneous ostensible justice and the connected concern that all participants in a war scrupulously observe the principle of restraint—in the case that their own cause was, after all, unjust.

There is a second problem with the aggressor–defender *jus ad bellum* of recent international law as viewed from the standpoint of just war tradition. Rather than concentrating solely on defense as the only allowable just cause for war, perhaps it is also necessary to keep in mind what Augustine saw clearly: that it is a moral duty for those who possess power to protect those who are relatively impotent when they are being threatened by others more powerful than they. This line of consideration means, I think, that we have a duty to construct our alliances so as to manifest our readiness to become involved in the defense of other peoples; it also implies that some cases may arise in which we have a duty to intervene even in the absence of specific treaties of alliance. The recognition of such a duty points in a direction diametrically opposite to the isolationist sentiments currently being voiced in some circles.

2. The requirement that every use of force be undertaken by *right authority* has traditionally served to legitimize the use of force by princes and, later, by states. In Augustine, to whom this term can be traced, "right authority" implies all the ends of good government. Rulers have their warmaking authority so that they can, acting in the stead of their people and on behalf of them, weigh the causes of war and decide whether they are just. But in the seventeenth century Grotius, by formalizing the criterion of just cause, opened the

way for a transformation of the criterion of right authority into the acceptance of state sovereignty. The modern idea of *compétence de guerre* resulted, by which a prince, as a man without master, could initiate war against another for whatever reasons he might consider just. At the same time persons without recognized sovereign authority possessed no such *compétence,* and resort to force by such persons could not properly be termed war or subjected to the limits of the law of war as it was then understood. This identification of the moral concept of right authority with the political concept of state sovereignty has made more problematic the question of how to make sense of the moral notion of authority in the contemporary world.

Perhaps more than any other just war concept, that of right authority may seem irrelevant to an age when so much cynicism exists about state power and in which, by contrast, popular revolutionary movements have for some persons taken on the presumption of legitimacy that formerly attached to the state. The historic function of the requirement that force be exercised by a *right* authority was chiefly to limit exactly the kind of unrestrained general violence and indiscriminate destruction that typically characterize civil wars. That is, this notion of right authority took on its classic meaning, building out of the base provided by Augustine, as a way of defining the police function of a coherent community of persons bound together under a commonly recognized authority, in opposition to the depredations of lawless individuals or bands of persons who challenged not only the ruling authority but the peace of the community itself.[9] This is the way, for example, that the late medieval canonists (for whom the criterion of right authority was clearly the preeminent just war category) used this idea: for them it was unambiguously a means of restricting resort to force and the destruction that the use of force invariably brings upon the lives and livelihoods of peaceful people.

At the very least this traditional moral criterion requires us today to apply the same standards to all uses of force, whatever their ostensible justifying cause and regardless of whether revolutionaries or representatives of the status quo are involved. The requirement that there must be a right authority for the use of force means that we must inquire whether there is any authority who can control the employment of force so as to limit its effects, and behind that to inquire as to the breadth and depth of popular support this authority possesses.[10]

3. The traditional requirement that use of force be the last resort bears in a particularly pointed way on contemporary affairs. We do not have a world government and are unlikely to have one in the foreseeable future, but we do have an international system manifesting a great deal of stability and—at least thus far—durability. In such a stable international environment the emphasis must be on relationships that do not involve the resort to forceful means. Fortunately, the tools of such relationships—diplomacy, economics, intellectual and cultural exchange—flourish in such an atmosphere, while the presumption is strongly against the initiation of a major war that by definition would mark the end of this era of stability. The same consideration does not apply to uses of forceful means at lower levels and in the service of diplomatic undertakings or other activities that fundamentally enhance stability. But the key concern is that the game must be worth the candle; even in such cases force must be the last step, not taken until other steps have been tried. The traditional idea that force must be the last resort thus carries with it the counsels of caution and prudence and serves as an implicit reminder that force may inspire more force, with the danger of loss of rational control over events. On the other hand, this criterion of *last* resort reminds us that the use of force may be a legitimate resort, when there are no other ways left to protect values that require to be preserved. Just war tradition thus points toward neither militarism nor pacifism, but to a state of affairs between these extremes.

The aggressor–defender *jus ad bellum* of contemporary international law tends to distort the last resort idea as well as that of just cause (as already seen). Where the right to use force is defined in sole terms of response to first use of force, the scales are weighted in advance in favor of adversaries who know how to use means such as subversion and third-party terrorism to gain their ends. The point is that the moment of last resort may come before the enemy fires its first shot across one's borders. What has been said above about the possibility, in certain kinds of instances, that a first use of force be a moral use also applies here. Whatever contemporary international law may say or be interpreted to say, the weight of Western moral tradition on war does not rule out that in some cases first use of force may appropriately be a response of last resort.

4. *Proportionality* as a moral principle applied to the restraint of war has two faces, having to do both with the original decision whether to use forceful means and with the multifold later decisions as to what levels or means of force are proper. Here I wish to speak about both of these ideas.

In *jus ad bellum* terms, the aim of the idea of proportionality is to ensure that the overall damage to human values that will result from the resort to force will be at least balanced evenly by the degree to which the same or other important values are preserved or protected. This "counting the costs" requires thinking into the future, and while such projection is notoriously risky, it must be done.

When we reflect on the proportionality or disproportionality of contemporary warfare in this sense of the idea, it is important to differentiate between the *destructive capability* of modern weapons and the *intentionality* that determines whether the most destructive means available will be used and, if so, how and in what context(s). These are distinct questions, and it is necessary for a genuinely moral weighing of the issue to divide them. World War II offers numerous examples of an intentionality aimed at producing indiscriminate mass destruction: the death camps and conventional countercity bombing long predated the atomic bomb. Without the precedents of London, Dresden, Hamburg, and Tokyo the obliteration of Hiroshima and Nagasaki would not have been thinkable. The kind of intentionality that led Vattel and others to question bombardment of cities with red-hot cannon balls and other incendiary means was emphatically lost in the total-war idea present in World War II, and it is this latter kind of intentionality that must morally be challenged no matter what sorts of weapons are available. Thus when we think of contemporary occasions when the use of force might be justified, the idea of proportionality requires that we think not only of the foreseeable results of the unlimited use of whatever weapons are available—whether nuclear, chemical, biological, or conventional. It requires also that we consider how workable and responsible limits may be imposed to make it possible to use forceful means to protect values that otherwise could not be preserved.

Modern-war pacifists generally overlook this distinction that must be made between intentionality and the destructive potential of weapons. This allows them to appeal to the "disproportionality" of modern weapons (and hence of modern war) as compared with any values that might be served by their employment. The most common form of this claim today is nuclear pacifism. Nuclear pacifists argue that whatever might have been said about the possibility of justice in war during earlier eras, today the use of nuclear weapons would necessarily result in a holocaust of unimaginable fury and horrifying impact. Their distortion of this moral concept of proportionality is that they deny the possibility of moral controls over the employment of forceful means. The tragic irony of this position is that it tends to remove nuclear weapons altogether from the sphere of human moral intentionality, so that the very end that is so dreadfully feared becomes the more possible: the holocaust that would result from an unlimited exchange of strategic nuclear weapons.

The purpose of thinking in just war terms, including the idea of proportionality as one of these terms, is to attempt to make rational moral decisions among possibilities that are available. Unless nuclear weapons, among all the others that are now available, are subordinated like all the others to a searching examination of the proper limits to human intentionality, we will have made a grave and potentially disastrous mistake.

This consideration leads naturally into the *jus in bello* meaning of the traditional concept of proportionality. At the very least, I would suggest, those persons are right who have advocated counterforce targeting of strategic nuclear weapons. This is one example of how human moral intentionality may be applied to define a restrained yet possibly rational use of such weaponry. The presumption against chemical and biological weapons is also rightly directed, for reasons having to do with discrimination or noncombatant protection as well as with proportionality, since such weapons tend both to be indiscriminate in use and to produce, more perhaps than nuclear weapons, long-term damage to human lives and values. In general, considerations of proportionality point us toward utilization of conventional weapons, whose effects can be predictably known and moderated; beyond that, such considerations point to the need to develop weapons of war that may be employed more proportionately than those now available. A moral obligation to use restraint in the protection of values implies developing means of war that can be employed with restraint, in the service of human intentionality. Thus the just war concept of proportionality drives toward two conclusions: that we forget the past intentionality that has conceived war as necessarily total and has nourished means of war that serve that conception, and further that we establish an intentionality of restraint and control over the weapons of war while fostering the development of new weapons that lend themselves to use in the service of such intentionality.

5. I have kept till last the wisdom preserved in the just war idea that noncombatants should be protected from the ravages of war. This idea of *noncombatant immunity*, also called the moral principle of *discrimination*, has been one of the strongest and most regular themes in just war tradition throughout its development, though it has not always been understood the same way. As stated forcefully by Paul Ramsey, for example, this idea is that noncombatants enjoy an absolute moral immunity from direct, intentional attack; but in the limited-war practice of the eighteenth century an equally powerful effort to protect noncombatants emerged, centered not on the immunity from harm of the individual but rather on restricting the theater of military operations so as not directly to threaten most of the inhabitants of bel-

ligerent nations. Here absolute immunity was defined geographically. The latter concept has again surfaced in some contemporary limited-war thought (that aimed at restricting the geographic scope of war), while contemporary humanitarian international law, like Ramsey, holds that certain classes of persons must be protected no matter where they are found. We are charged with remembering that noncombatants are indeed morally different from combatants, and that our behavior toward them in wartime must accordingly be different. Warfare in which combatants and noncombatants are perceived and treated as essentially alike is fundamentally against the major moral tradition of war in Western culture.

Yet powerful forces in the modern world have tended to suppress the memory of this moral obligation to protect noncombatants. Nowhere is the result of this suppression more obvious than in a strategic nuclear policy that threatens population centers rather than military forces that (I should think presumably) represent the real enemy in wartime. But the evil is not limited to such strategic targeting or to the actions of nation-states; when terrorists choose as their preferred targets persons who have no perceptible connection to the exercise of power or to the military use of force—and the more disconnected from power the victims are, the more successful the terrorism—we have an equally glaring case of the immorality of a conception of the use of force that does not recognize the moral duty not to harm noncombatants.

The moral requirement to protect noncombatants implies the development of weapons usable in ways that satisfy legitimate military functions without corollary damage to the lives, livelihoods, and property of noncombatants. In the fourteenth century the noble monk Honoré Bonet, writing of the law of war in his own time, put this in homely terms: warriors were not to use their arms on peaceful peasants, merchants, or others as they went about their business, nor on the ox of the peasant nor the ass that carried the merchant's wares. These were neither of the knightly class (that is, they were not socialized as soldiers), nor were they functioning in warlike ways; they ought as a moral duty to be left alone, not only in their lives but in their property.[11] Such a moral consideration has important implications for future weapons development, as well as for the debate over such new weapons as the neutron bomb, the cruise missile, MX, and other components of contemporary military policy.

Conclusion

I have been arguing in this chapter for the contemporary relevance of the moral ideas developed and preserved in just war tradition and known by reflection on that tradition. These ideas represent, I have argued, the only way actually open for persons in our culture to think about morality and war. At the very least they represent formal criteria for our thinking, questions that we must ask whenever we begin to think seriously about the possibility of using forceful means to protect important values. But beyond this purely formal set of questions, I have suggested further that there is wisdom present in the content given to these ideas in our historical tradition of moral judgment on war, and that reflection on that wisdom will help to keep us from making mistakes in our contemporary efforts to answer the questions of whether and how we might justifiably employ force in the protection of important values. In sum, I have been arguing that just war tradition provides us with three fundamental moral reminders: first, that sometimes the use of force may be necessary to protect or preserve values that would otherwise be damaged or lost; second, that both the resort to force and the application of forceful means must be subjected to a searching intentionality of justification and restraint; and third, that means and methods of war should be developed so as to serve the legitimate moral purposes of the employment of force in international affairs.

2

Can Contemporary Armed Conflicts Be Just?

As we have already seen, justice in the just war sense can refer either to the decision to employ force or to the decision as to what kinds and/or degrees of force to employ. Often in the historical development of Western moral tradition on war it has been argued that the question whether to use force takes logical priority over the question of what force to use and conditions it: thus in the sixteenth century Franciscus de Victoria reasoned that during a siege undertaken in a just war it was morally permissible to use weapons that, because of the indiscriminate character of the destruction they caused, would endanger noncombatants;[1] similarly the contemporary theorist Michael Walzer has described the argument from supreme emergency as a rationale for utilizing means of war that would otherwise be prohibited for moral reasons.[2] In both of these cases the justice of the cause was allowed to override the justice of the particular means used to serve that cause; noncombatant protection in particular, and perhaps the idea of proportionality as well, thus lost their effectiveness as restraints on the destructiveness of war. This amounts to making a moral priority out of a logical one. At the other extreme, modern-war pacifists of various persuasions have often used an argument from proportionality to condemn all use of military means in the service of political goals:[3] the weapons of modern war, their argument goes, are destructive out of all proportion to any values they might serve; therefore resort to force can never any more be justified as a political instrument. This sort of argument was directed against the war in Vietnam; more generally it is typical of the nuclear pacifist position. This line of reasoning admits, at least in theory, that force might in some conditions be employed in the service of values—to protect and preserve them, if not to advance them. But it moves quickly to the empirical judgment that those conditions do not now obtain.

In these two assignments of priority we have, in fact, two extremes in moral reasoning about war. While they must be taken seriously, since they represent serious efforts at drawing conclusions about particular situations on the basis of moral values integral to the tradition of just war, both of them in their extremity give up too much from that tradition. Victoria recognized this by balancing his argument about the priority of just cause with the observation that both sides in a conflict might seem to have equally just causes, so that neither had the freedom to fight unrestrainedly; rather, he argued, both were constrained to scrupulous observance of the *jus in bello* limits.[4] Walzer too undercuts the supreme emergency argument by showing it to be finally a kind of evil, though undertaken in the service of good.[5] Both these theorists, along with the main line of Western moral tradition on war generally, have in their reasoning about war pushed toward the center rather than toward the extreme; the final message is not that just cause inevitably takes priority over just, restrained conduct of war but rather that a balance must be kept between considerations of whether to use force and of how to use it.[6] For this reason we must avoid the opposite extreme as well, that of the modern-war pacifist. In this position too the balance is lost, and along with it an important part of our historical moral wisdom about the use of force in human affairs. The lesson lost from that wisdom is that in life as we know it, it is sometimes necessary to oppose evil by force unless evil is to triumph. The purpose of the balance between the *ad bellum* and *in bello* sense of justice in Western moral tradition is to recognize this simple fact about human history and yet to manage the use of force so that it does not come to represent in itself a greater evil than the evil it is used to correct. If the judgment is made for the case of war in the modern age that we have somehow passed over a threshold, so that the use of force does now represent that greater evil, then—quite apart from the question whether that judgment is correct—the next step for those convinced by such reasoning should be to seek other ways—morally acceptable, humanly usable ways—to combat the value-destroying forces of evil effectively. This too points us back toward the center, toward the restoration of balance, toward holding fast to both the *jus ad bellum* and the *jus in bello* senses of justice regarding the employment of force.

Ends thus have to be held in mind when speaking of means, and means when speaking of ends. This needs to be said explicitly because the discussion in the rest of this chapter is organized around categories defined by different means of war. This does not indicate that I believe the question of ends has already been answered, only that if we are able to discover, for any of these contemporary cases, that the use of force is a moral possibility in the *jus in bello* sense, the decision about the right ends for which to use such force may then be made in good conscience—since the decision to use force when there are no morally acceptable means of force available is not a morally conscientious decision. Indeed, it may be helpful to read the following discussion as an acceptance of the challenge posed above to the modern-war pacifist: beginning with a presupposition that the contemporary use of force carries with it the specter of great destruction and human suffering, the problem is whether any possible uses of force can be identified or defined that could serve moral ends. I believe they can, but I believe also that restraints must be imposed on the use of force even in the service of moral ends. Some possible uses of force must be denied because they are so at odds with the moral values they are ostensibly meant to protect. Understanding these moral restraints on means of force in several types of contemporary war is our present concern. I will return to the problem of ends that appear to justify unrestrained force in chapter 8 below.

In the following I will proceed by identifying, then commenting upon, five types of possible contemporary armed conflict. There may be others, but these five present the most pressing problems. The first three represent gradations in possible conflicts between or among established, recognized states; the last two involve parties who stand outside the sphere of political legitimacy in some way. Most of Western tradition on justifying and restraining the use of force has had to do with the former kind of conflict, as symbolized in international law—a major carrier of this tradition—where the term *war* has denoted a formally defined and declared state of hostilities between or among international persons, the established states. But there is no good reason to restrict the application of the tradition in such a way as this, and in the contemporary world to do so would result in an ostrichlike avoidance of the fact of revolutionary warfare of various sorts, as well as the pressing issue of terrorism. Again symbolically, international lawyers have turned to the phrase *armed conflict* as a replacement for the formal state of war in their discipline, attempting to find a mechanism for applying the restraints contained in the international law of war to this broader arena of armed conflicts, where at least one of the actors is not a nation-state. Similarly, in what follows I will employ just war tradition to examine each of the kinds of contemporary armed conflicts identified, though (unlike the practice in international law) I will use the terms *war* and *armed conflict* interchangeably, meaning by both the use of force for ends of a political nature by groups of people sufficiently united to be able to agree upon such ends.

The five types of contemporary armed conflict I will discuss are as follows; in my discussion of each I will proceed both generally and by examining a particular case exemplifying the type of conflict being treated:

1. War between the superpowers (the United States and the Soviet Union and their respective allies) involving strategic nuclear weapons.

2. War involving the use of nuclear weapons of the tactical/theater variety.
3. Wars between established powers involving the use of conventional weapons only.
4. Insurgency or revolutionary conflict involving conventional weapons.
5. Terrorism as a means of war in the pursuit of political goals.

Taken as a group, these five categories define an inverted pyramid in terms of the numbers of persons and the level of destruction threatened by each of the types of conflict. This does not mean that those farther down the list are any the less dangerous as threats to values. Terrorism, for example, is of a piece with counterpopulation nuclear strategy in depending on harm or the threat of harm directed toward innocent persons; these two disparate means of contemporary war thus equally ignore and undermine the moral concern to protect noncombatants, one of the principal values evolved in Western moral tradition on war. Indeed, in terms of the frequency of occurrence, terrorism might be argued to represent the greater threat to this human value, since it has become a constant reality in some societies and some conflicts, while counterpopulation strategic nuclear war remains only a much-feared possibility.

Another relationship exists among the types of contemporary conflict as I have listed them. In conventional wars between established national powers, we have the kind of conflict around which most of just war tradition has coalesced; this, then, is a kind of center or core, and on either side are examples of steps away from this center that have become significant forms of conflict in the contemporary world. In thinking whether contemporary armed conflicts can be just, it is necessary to relate the kinds of conflict on either side of the center back to what we know from just war tradition about the limits of justified force in conventional wars between established national political units. So my listing of the five kinds of contemporary armed conflict is not simply random; it is meant as a reminder that in practical moral reasoning we must measure what we do not know by what we know. In this case what we know about the ideals of political responsibility expressed in the concept of nation-state and the ideals of limitation, direction, and restraint in the use of force for political purposes must be extended to both sides so as to be brought into relation with contemporary reality: on the one side, the breakdown of humanly controllable and restrainable force; on the other, the breakdown of that notion of politics in which the political unit serves the goods of persons and not those defined in an abstract ideology. To define such a relation of Western moral tradition on war to these extremes is the substantial task before us when we confront the question of justice in contemporary war.

Strategic Nuclear War: The Superpower Confrontation

The possibility of strategic nuclear war between the superpowers has been the subject of a long history of debate reaching back now for more than thirty years. At the same time the destructive potential of the strategic nuclear arsenals has grown enormously. The strategic force is designed for deterrence rather than use; yet for the deterrent effect to be realistic, the threat of use of the weapons must be perceived as not an empty one. Thus we need to take seriously the possibility for use of strategic nuclear weapons and, at the extreme, the possibility of an all-out exchange of such weapons in a superpower war.

By the standards of just war tradition, it is only at the limits of reason—and perhaps not even there—that this extreme kind of war could be thought of as just. It is difficult to imagine how anyone who begins seriously from the purpose of protecting or preserving values by the use of force could regard *this* use of force, so enormously destructive of values and so indiscriminate (whether designedly so or not) in its effects, as an appropriate means. Indeed, those individuals who have tried to think about nuclear war of this sort (as, for example, theologians Paul Ramsey and John Courtney Murray) have consistently taken the opposite position,[7] as have the mass of persons of more more modest theoretical abilities and less thoroughly developed schemes of moral analysis.

Why, then, do we continue to possess a strategic nuclear arsenal, and not only to possess it but to add to it? The answer offered by a host of strategic theorists who stress the need for nuclear force stability is foremost its perceived deterrent power: there have been no wars involving the superpowers in direct conflict with each other since the nuclear age began. Though international stability through nuclear deterrence is dangerous, it has proven durable.[8] A second major factor is that no clear path exists to the removal of dependence on strategic nuclear weapons for the purpose they serve. One-sided escalation or disarmament tends to produce strategic instability. Similarly, modes of targeting of the strategic weapons other than the threat of all-out counterpopulation use tends, in the minds of many strategic analysts, to weaken the effectiveness of the deterrent, thus increasing the likelihood of nuclear war. In their view, the risk of nuclear war is lessened by increasing the likelihood of mutual mass annihilation should nuclear weapons be used.

There are, however, two reasons why it is necessary to move beyond this stage in thinking about strategic nuclear weapons. The first is that the game of deterrence is largely a game dependent on perception. If the threat is of such a nature as to make carrying it out utterly irrational, then it loses its force. In the context of present strategic discussion, this concern takes shape in the argument that an irrationally destructive deterrent force deters only an equally irrational destructive force, leaving untouched the possibility of use of force at lower levels. While neither superpower would want to risk almost certain annihilation of its own major population centers and its industrial base by a countercity strike against the other, some form of limited nuclear weapons use might well take place, particularly if the targets were the nuclear forces of the other side. The fact that the possibility of such nuclear war as this is being considered is one reason we need to give attention to it here. The other reason comes directly out of considerations based in just war tradition. If the all-out use of strategic nuclear weapons is morally condemned, we must ask whether and how other possible uses of nuclear weaponry can be morally judged. In the nuclear context this leads us immediately to the question of counter-force warfare.

Even in the rarefied region of strategic weapons inter-change there are some ways of using these weapons that are worse than others. A countercity strike would be a direct and intentional attack against noncombatants, representing a violation of noncombatant immunity on a mass scale—this besides anything we might say about the disproportionality of such destruction as a countercity strike would entail. Paul Ramsey has developed the moral argument against such use of nuclear weapons more fully than any other analyst over the generation of debate we have now had,[9] and for him it is this concern for the rights of noncombatants, this violation of the moral principle of discrimination, that removes all possibility that a direct, intentional countercity attack could be a moral use of force. This drives Ramsey toward accep-tance of counterforce targeting, even with the recognition that such targeting may produce harm to noncombatants and disproportionate destruction. Counterforce targeting represents at least a move in the right direction. More re-cently political scientist Bruce Russett has sketched a posi-tion similar to Ramsey's that depends finally on a commit-ment to the moral conception of discrimination but stresses the strategic–pragmatic reasons for counterforce targeting.[10] Russett in this essay exemplifies those contemporary nu-clear strategists who argue for counterforce targeting as creating a more credible deterrent than countercity target-ing does. His reasoning is that an announced intention on the part of the United States to destroy the Soviet Union's power to resist a conventional invasion—particularly an in-vasion by China on the long border shared by those two powers—would be both more moral and more believable as a statement of actual intent than a deterrence policy ori-ented wholly to the announced intent to strike Soviet popu-lation centers. This essentially pragmatic argument thus complements Ramsey's effort to think through the implica-tions of what he conceives to be an absolute moral principle, discrimination.

From the standpoint of just war tradition, neither sort of

argument represents more than a negative preference, a ranking of less evil use of strategic nuclear weapons over more evil ones. Choosing the lesser evil does not always amount to choosing the greater good, and in this case it must be questioned whether counterforce use of strategic nuclear weapons could be justified from the perspective of the need morally to protect and preserve values through force.

Let us consider in particular the argument made by Ramsey, which rests on the principle that it is always wrong directly and intentionally to harm noncombatants. Even in a counterforce or designedly countercombatant use of nuclear weapons of strategic magnitude, it is impossible to separate out the expectation of harm to noncombatants. Employing the rule of double effect, Ramsey argues that so long as such harm is not "direct and intentional," it is morally permissible. The difficulty with his use of this moral rule in the case of strategic nuclear weapons lies in their enormous destructive effect, which is foreknown and can be calculated for a given target. If a terrorist is holding a group of innocent persons prisoner in a house threatening to kill them, it is correct to argue that it would be moral for a sniper to attempt to kill the terrorist first by a rifle shot, even though he might miss and kill one of the hostages or the bullet might kill the terrorist but pass through his body to kill a hostage as well. It would not be correct use of the argument from double effect to argue that it would be moral to blow up the house with TNT, knowing that the terrorist would be killed but that all the hostages would perish as well. Yet this latter is exactly the kind of case before us when we consider the effects of strategic nuclear weapons. There is also the problem of whether we count only the immediate or also the long-term effects of the weapon used, and since nuclear weapons produce persistent radioactivity to menace persons entering the target area for many years after the blast, I am convinced that we must also count this threat among the challenges to the immunity of noncombatants. After any war all persons are noncombatants, and use of weapons that will foreseeably endanger generations yet unborn by making target areas unlivably "hot" represents as much a violation of noncombatancy as a bullet through the brain of a child held hostage to cause an enemy to surrender.

In short, while we must grant that it is morally necessary and appropriate to consider less evil possibilities for use of strategic nuclear weapons than countercity targeting represents, still the idea of counterforce targeting requires that we press further. Various levels of limited employment of weapons of strategic magnitude, all of which might fall under the rubric of counterforce or countercombatant targeting, ought to be considered and ranked in a hierarchy of preferability that would define the order of intended use. But even leaving aside the "firebreak" argument (that any use of nuclear weapons would lead to escalation right up to an all-out strategic exchange), there exist significant moral reasons against even the lowest levels of such countercombatant use, reasons that gain strength the farther up the escalation ladder one proceeds. Current strategic nuclear weapons are simply too grossly destructive to be employed with restraint in nearly any conceivable military situation, and their use even against a legitimate (that is, a combatant) target would entail such foreseeable collateral harm to noncombatants as to cast grave doubt on the morality of such use.

In a subsequent chapter I will return to this question of nuclear strategy for deterrence and potential use, taking up in more detail the possibility of some form of limited targeting as a moral strategic posture in the nuclear age.

Moral concern has tended to focus too exclusively at the extreme possibility of war involving an all-out exchange of the strategic weaponry of the superpowers. No particular intelligence or moral sensitivity is required to recognize that such an exchange would be very gravely wrong. To call it wrong thus does not really get us anywhere, even if it might have done so once. Rather it is now time we focused our concerns on how to avoid this kind of use that is so generally agreed to be wrong. Several avenues for further exploration can be identified, all of which I will treat in one way or other later in this book. First, there is the problem of how to use the strategic weapons we now have, should we ever have to employ them, in the least evil ways. This is the question of counterforce targeting in its many theoretical manifestations. Second, there is the question of how to ensure that the deterrent force remains a deterrent, never having to be actually employed. Third, there is the problem of what might possibly—and more morally—replace reliance on nuclear weapons in both strategy and tactics. This overlaps with the question of counterforce targeting in that both point in the direction of developing more accurate, less individually destructive, less indiscriminate nuclear weapons and beyond that to the development and use of other kinds of weapons in the place of nuclear ones.

War Involving Tactical/Theater Nuclear Weapons: NATO vs. Warsaw Pact Forces in Europe

While tactical and theater nuclear weapons are not identical, together they present, for the purposes of moral analysis at least, substantially different problems and possibilities from those presented by strategic nuclear weapons. Just as the enormous destructive capability and the doctrine according to which they are targeted make it difficult or perhaps impossible to think of the moral use of strategic weapons in war, so the lower destructive capability and the doctrine defining the use of tactical and theater weapons bring them into the conceptual range where it is meaningful to think about conflicts in which these latter sorts of weapons might possibly be the ones of moral choice. These are designedly the weapons of limited nuclear war, and if such a war can fall within the scope of the moral restraints shaped in just war tradition, it is far more likely to be the one in which these sorts of weapons are used and not the strategic type—even if the latter are used only sparingly and not in an all-out spasm of mutual annihilation. The other side of this consideration is that while the fundamental purpose of strategic nuclear weapons is deterrence, not use, the priorities are reversed for tactical and theater nuclear weapons. This is not to say that the latter have no particular function as deterrents to war, but that their nature, intended targets, and modes of delivery all are defined by the assumption that they would be in fact used in a war, given certain conditions. It is sometimes argued that this likelihood for use makes tactical and theater nuclear weapons the best deterrents; I find this persuasive, but the opposite position is that such weapons as this are unnecessary given the existence of the strategic deterrent forces, and the issue remains in debate.

Definitionally it is most useful to think of the terms *strategic, theater,* and *tactical* as representing points along a spectrum when applied to describe nuclear weapons. That there is definitional and conceptual overlap, especially in the middle of the spectrum, where the term *theater* is found, is one of the reasons why nuclear arms control is so difficult to achieve: one nation's theater weapons may appear strategic to a potential enemy, and tactical ones may appear to be of the theater type or even, at the extreme, strategic. This problem of overlap is also one reason why many persons remain convinced of the truth of the firebreak concept: that the similarities among all the types of nuclear weapons are such, and the differences between them taken collectively and conventional weapons are such, that any use of a nuclear weapon of whatever sort would likely lead to escalation to an all-out strategic interchange. Nonetheless, it is possible to distinguish these types of nuclear weapons from each other; red light is different from violet, though both are colors of the visible spectrum, and orange can be distinguished from red even though they lie next to each other in the spectrum of colors of light. For nuclear weapons this distinction can be made by thinking of the European theater, where all three types of nuclear weapons may be found along with conventional ones, and which figures most prominently in scenarios of limited nuclear war. In these scenarios the so-called homelands of the United States and the Soviet Union are separated from the theater of war, which is defined as including the NATO and Warsaw Pact nations of Western Europe, while the actual battlefield where tactical nuclear weapons may be used is a much smaller geographical area, typically thought of as principally in West German territory.[11] In this situation the tactical nuclear weapons are those meant for use against specific concentrations of combatants, such as a tank advance; theater weapons are those intended for use against such targets as staging areas behind the lines of actual battle, where the intended targets would still be first of all military forces; and strategic weapons are what is left: the high-yield, missile- or bomber-delivered weapons targeted on the national homelands of the superpowers and intended in many cases as counterpopulation, not countercombatant or counterforce, weapons. Here the fundamental moral distinctions have to do with the size of each broad type of weapon and the intended target of each. The lower yield of weapons toward the tactical end of the spectrum makes them inherently more useful in morally proportionate ways, while their countercombatant targeting marks them as intentionally more morally discriminate. These are important distinctions, and I shall return to them below.

We need not think of tactical and theater nuclear weapons only in terms of possible conflict in Europe; such weapons can in principle be employed anywhere, and in particular the size and portability of tactical nuclear warheads makes them especially attractive for mating to cruise missiles of indeterminate range and to tactical aircraft. But the NATO–Warsaw Pact confrontation in Europe remains the paradigmatic case, and the particular weapons systems available to both sides have been fashioned with the circumstances of a possible European war foremost in mind. Limited nuclear war scenarios, as already noted, have also typically dealt with this case. Thus good reasons exist for beginning moral analysis here, though as will be seen the possibilities for a moral use of nuclear weapons in this context are extremely limited.

I will focus basically upon the two key questions of the means of war in just war tradition: discrimination and proportionality. That is, would tactical and/or theater nuclear weapons, while designedly countercombatant or counterforce weapons, pose a threat to noncombatants, both present and future, in such a densely populated theater of war? If so, what kinds of weapons and what conditions for their use work to diminish or eliminate this threat? Further, would the level of damage caused by these sorts of weapons lie within the range where they do not create more evil than they prevent or remedy? What may be said about the nature of these weapons and their particular use so as to maximize the prospect of their proportionate use? These are questions to be asked of every weapon, every tactic, every strategy of war, and they must in succeeding sections of this chapter be asked of non-nuclear armed conflicts. For now, though, we will attempt to bracket those broader concerns in order to sharpen what must be said morally about the possibility of limited nuclear war involving tactical/theater weapons.

First, though, the firebreak argument must be dealt with. If it is correct, then the whole concept of limited nuclear war is chimerical. This argument has two aspects, the first of which is that the effects of conventional and nuclear weapons can be distinguished from each other under battlefield conditions—at least in theory—while nuclear weapons are difficult to distinguish from one another in the context of battle. A low-yield tactical blast close up, it is argued, may appear much like a medium-yield theater blast farther off, while either one may appear to a nervous observer to be or to portend the detonation of a high-yield strategic warhead. On the other hand, by depending on the quality of battlefield observations this argument ignores the fact that satellite observation is capable of identifying both the location of a nuclear explosion and its yield quite precisely; if information from such observation is available, neither potential belligerent will have to depend on some colonel—or some corporal in a forward observation post—peering through binoculars at a mushroom cloud and trying to guess where and how large the detonation was.

In general, then, this response to the first part of the firebreak argument depends on the continuing availability during a battle for control of Western Europe of information from sophisticated intelligence-gathering systems, of which satellites are the most important. But this response also depends on the maintenance of command authority over nuclear weapons at a level high enough to weigh both the general military and the political consequences of employing such weapons; it depends on restricting control over those weapons so as to guarantee, so far as possible, that they will be used only in accord with the decisions of the higher command authority; and it depends on the continued existence under battle conditions of a secure line of communications between this higher authority and the battlefield commanders who actually have the tactical/theater nuclear weapons in their possession. Morally speaking, there is an advance responsibility to frame policy for tactical/theater weapons use that would keep the decision for such use centralized at the highest levels of political and military command; beyond this, the problem becomes one of what military people call C^3I: how to maintain command authority, secure control and communications, and good intelligence about what is actually taking place. The first aspect of the firebreak argument represents the judgment that under the "fog of war" C^3I will break down and lower-level officers will act hastily and ill-advisedly to shoot off nuclear weapons in their possession. The response to it represents a contrary judgment; yet more than that, it represents the conscious effort to meet the objections to tactical/theater nuclear weapons raised from this side of the firebreak argument. So far as the decision to employ such weapons is reserved to the highest levels and not dispersed to lower-grade officers in the field, and so far as good, secure C^3I is maintained, this side of the firebreak argument is unconvincing.

The other part of the argument raises the question of perception. It may be, in fact, advantageous to a belligerent not to be entirely clear whether he will escalate toward the strategic end of the spectrum when he employs the first tactical nuclear warhead. Yet it is precisely where such ambiguity exists that the firebreak argument against use of any kind of nuclear weapons is strongest. This suggests that, in spite of the tactical advantages of ambiguity, belligerents should attempt to make quite clear in whatever ways available their intention that the use of nuclear weapons be limited to a specific level. Because of the overlap between strategic and theater weapons, the specific level chosen should as clearly as possible be on the tactical side of the spectrum of possibilities (though this may include some theater weapons use). If this is not the course chosen, the firebreak argument against use of nuclear weapons in war may not wisely be disregarded.

A related issue is, of course, whether the most important firebreak is the outbreak of *any* sort of war.[12] The experience of the world wars seems to teach that once war breaks out, escalation to the maximum military capability of each belligerent is only a matter of time. So far as this outcome is feared, it tends to reinforce deterrence, and it is possible that this firebreak is the only significant one where the superpowers are concerned. Essentially this concept of firebreak—that any war inevitably leads to all-out escalation—denies the validity of the limited war idea in the contemporary age. But ample historical evidence shows limited war in our own time to be a genuine option, so long as at least one of the parties directly involved is not the United States or the Soviet Union or their principal allies.[13] The problem, then, is what would happen should an armed conflict erupt with these two sides as the adversaries. No one knows, frankly, whether it would be possible to keep such a war limited, or whether the pressures to escalate would lead inexorably to an all-out conflict involving the use of strategic nuclear weapons. But given the accidental nature of the outbreak of many wars, including some of the bloodiest, it would be foolish not to think carefully in advance about the sorts of limitations that should obtain and to take steps to incorporate them in the military defense posture. Otherwise the expectation that any war must be a total war becomes self-fulfilling prophecy.

Strategic nuclear weapons pose moral problems because of both their capability for disproportionate destruction of values and the near impossibility of reasonably eliminating harm to noncombatants. In judging the weapons of limited nuclear war we need to question whether these same moral problems obtain here also. And as in the case of strategic weapons we need to take account of the long-term harm that is done, affecting human lives, property, and other values after the war is over, when all are noncombatants.

In the past, the tactical nuclear weapons that both NATO and Warsaw Pact forces have had available have been fission warheads whose yield is low only by contrast to that of thermonuclear (fusion) strategic weapons and that are by their nature too radioactively "dirty" to be used with any reasonable hope of discrimination. Given the density of population in Western Europe, any war in which these weapons were employed—even if no larger nuclear weapons were used—would have been a crime against noncombatants, and the resultant destruction would have been disproportionate. The point is that in such a theater of war it is impossible to discriminate in using such weapons between their foreknowable (and desired) effects on combatants and their equally foreknowable (but undesired) effects on noncombatants. Morally this case is the same whether the noncombatants harmed are one's own population or the enemy's, but politically the situation is worsened because, in fighting among one's own population, such weapons would destroy the very lives and values they were meant ideally to protect. This would be absurd. So this case turns out to present us with the same sort of problems we encountered in discussing strategic nuclear weapons, and the answer must be the same: only at the limits of reason could such a war be morally possible.

But now let us consider the effect of changing the type of battlefield nuclear weapons available; specifically, let us consider whether introducing the neutron warhead into NATO to replace the older fission warheads would make a moral difference. I believe it does, at least given certain conditions regarding its use, and I shall have more to say about those conditions in chapter 5 below; at present, though, I will sketch what is at stake morally in the contrast between these two types of weapons.

The neutron warhead is a fusion, not fission, device; that is, it is a low-yield version of the thermonuclear weapons that make up the strategic forces of the nuclear powers. The yield, or explosive power, of the neutron warhead is described as comparable to that of the fission warheads it replaces. Now, given a particular yield and particular conditions for use, it is characteristic of fusion weapons that they are radioactively "cleaner" than fission weapons, both in the types of short-run radiation produced and in terms of lingering, residual radiation of low but significant magnitude. At the same time, the ratio of total immediate radiation effect to blast produced is much higher for the fusion than for the fission warhead. This last consideration is the root of the familiar description of the neutron warhead as one that kills people—ideally, enemy soldiers—but leaves property relatively undamaged. That property is left undamaged, whether by blast or by lingering radiation, is significant for protecting the rights of noncombatants, who must have buildings in which to live, work, and shop, means of transportation, land to farm, and so on. The neutron warhead is definitely superior morally to tactical fission warheads in these terms; it is both more inherently discriminate and more proportionate. In terms of the immediate effects of each type of weapon, the most that can be said is that the *potential* for greater discrimination and proportionate use exists in the neutron warhead, so that in some circumstances it may even be the weapon of moral choice over conventional explosives (which also may be judged relative to the concepts of discrimination and proportionality). But these circumstances need to be spelled out, and that is the purpose of my discussion below in chapter 5 on weapons and tactics.

Meanwhile, there remains the problem that even if the neutron warhead completely replaced fission warheads in NATO, Warsaw Pact forces would still have only fission weapons. It is unrealistic to suppose that use of a fusion device would not evoke response by means of a fission device. So the final result, a Carthaginian peace, might well be the same; only the burden of principal responsibility would be shifted. This would likely provide only limited comfort to the survivors of such a limited nuclear war and help those who did not survive not at all. A limited nuclear war in Western Europe or in any other similarly densely populated area thus appears to remain, at best, only at the edge of moral possibility.

Wars between Established Powers Using Conventional Weapons: The Falklands War of 1982

If we were to look at the case of a war in Western Europe using conventional weapons only, we might well still have to reach the negative conclusion forced when we were considering a limited nuclear war there. Contemporary conventional weaponry has great destructive capability, and there is more than enough of it between NATO and Warsaw Pact forces to produce devastation of European society even apart from the use of nuclear weapons. The results of the two world wars are our guides, and while the aim of stopping Hitler may cogently be held to justify the destruction of World War II, World War I is another matter entirely, where the destructive effects in the end totally outweighed the reasonable causes adduced to justify the conflict at its beginning. Still, conventional weaponry is by its nature more capable of discriminate and proportionate use than the nuclear weapons now available, as well as perhaps less likely to produce escalation to strategic missile exchange. Thus where Western Europe is concerned, the aim of defense preparation should be to maximize reliance on effective conventional weaponry to reduce the possibility of resort to nuclear weapons. Even so, the danger posed by a European war using whatever kinds of weapons remains so grave that here a virtual imperative to avoid war exists.

But limited conventional wars remain as a real if regrettable feature of international life in other areas of the world, and they have erupted in various forms over the four decades since the end of World War II. A limited war is not, in and of itself, a morally justified war, either in its ends or in its means, though a precondition to the moral use of force must be an intentionality of restraint.[14] In this section and the following one I shall briefly examine two cases of limited war in our immediate history, both of which employed conventional weaponry only, asking what may be said about the justice of each in just war terms.

The Falklands war between Britain and Argentina is the first case I will treat: a conventional war between established powers, fought for limited goals and marked by the use of limited means and restraint in the conduct of hostilities. This is a relatively easy war to describe in traditional just war terms. While the state of war was never formally declared by either side, the conflict was authorized by the governing officials in each country and was under their control; similarly, the aims of each were made publicly clear.[15] The result of this conflict has been, at least for the present, the *status quo ante bellum,* which if not identical with the just war criterion "the end of peace" has for practical purposes replaced it in international law. Was the use of force a last resort? The British can reasonably claim that it was, since the Argentine government refused to remove its troops from the Falklands even after intense negotiations and international pressure. An Argentine claim that force was a last resort for them is not believable; rather, their military occupation of the islands stands out instead as an act of opportunism. This sense that the opportunity was there shows that the Argentine government judged it had a reasonable hope of success in its actions; similarly, the ability to project force over long distances gave the British government confidence of its success.

So far as the *jus ad bellum* concepts are concerned, this leaves us with the questions of just cause and right intent, which cannot easily be distinguished in this case. Together they require a somewhat closer look.

Historically there have been three broad concepts of when use of military force is justified between powers: in defense of one's own, or under certain circumstances others', rights against an aggression that is in progress; in attempting to recover something that has earlier, because of another's aggression, been taken away; or to punish another for unjust aggressive acts already committed.[16] The fundamental idea in all three is defense: in the first case we have what was classically called incontinent defense, the attempt to parry the aggressor's upraised sword; in the latter two we have responses against acts already completed, against a sword that has already fallen. The difference between them is what has been lost as a result: persons and/or property, in the second historical formula, and ideas or principles in the third. In the Falklands war these latter two justifying rationales were employed by both sides, with both sides claiming also defense of their own rights, and by extension those of other nations. The Argentine claim was principally to be acting to recover lost territory: the Falklands had been taken from Argentina by the British a hundred and fifty years earlier. But there was also an undertone, which grew louder in the propaganda war as it developed, of punishment of colonialism. On the British side the claim to be acting to recover what was lost was also made strongly and with more immediate evidence in its favor: the islands had been British territory for a century and a half, and the inhabitants were British through and through. But Prime Minister Thatcher and her representatives also made much of the need to punish military aggression, so that Argentina's action in seizing the Falklands could not become a model for other aggressive states desiring their neighbors' territory.

Because of the century and a half of British rule and the British citizenship of the islands' inhabitants, the Argentine claim to be fighting to recover its own was anemic from the first. Similarly, its invocation of the evils of colonialism did not carry the ring of truth: this was something of an afterthought bearing the accent rather of propaganda than of reality. Similarly, Argentina's attempt to represent itself as an example of a third world country being put upon by imperialism contrasted sharply with the earlier Argentine tendency to align itself with the powers and cultures of the northern hemisphere rather than with the southern. The British arguments were, by contrast, much stronger and fitted the facts better. Just cause, as measured by external signs through political judgment, lay rather with Britain than with Argentina.

Intent by itself is a matter of morality rather than political judgment; yet alongside political claims, to understand intent is a necessary element in appraising the nature and validity of those claims. Augustine, who first injected considerations of intent into just war analysis, identified wrong intention with "the desire for harming, the cruelty of avenging, an unruly and implacable animosity, the rage of rebellion, the lust of domination and the like."[17] He might have added Machiavelli's counsel from *The Prince:* in order to head off disunity at home, start a foreign war.[18] In the context of Argentine politics, the seizure of the Falklands was classically Machiavellian. But was either side really guilty of wrong intent as described by Augustine? The answer has to be no, precisely because the armed conflict itself, as it developed in May and June of 1982, was so measured and restrained and was consciously limited to the geographical area around the Falklands. The danger inherent in the concept of justified punishment is that such punishment may get out of hand; it did not do so in the Falklands dispute. While Britain had the juster cause, both Argentina and Britain fought as if they did and as if they were bound by the just war rules of conflict.[19] This bears out what I have been arguing about the nature of just war tradition as the repository for consensual moral wisdom, crossing national boundaries within the scope of the broader cultural consciousness, regarding the use of military force.

Let us quickly look at the matter of how this war was fought, raising the issues of proportionality and discrimination. By contrast with Western Europe, the Falklands are a sparsely populated region, that many islanders took the opportunity to leave given them by Argentina after the initial takeover reduced the number of noncombatants in the islands still further. Some of the remaining persons dispersed to remote areas. Others, though, were left in the towns, which naturally became the sites where land battles occurred. Yet both sides in the conflict respected the civilians' noncombatant rights, and accordingly casualties among them were small. Partly this was the result of the fact that much of the fighting took place at sea or in the air; partly it resulted from the types of weapons used, which were inherently capable of discriminating use, and the tactics employed, which were countercombatant tactics only. Both sides possessed the capability of employing more force than they used; both had weapons of much greater mass destructive potential than were employed in the land warfare; and bloodier tactics for use of the forces available could easily have been adopted, creating more casualties among soldiers and civilians alike. Finally, the war might have been widened: British bombers had the capability to strike the Argentine mainland, and Argentine submarines or other naval vessels might have moved against the British troopships as they steamed down the South Atlantic. Beyond these measures, terrorist tactics might have been employed against the population of either country. Such widening of war in both geography and methods is expected as inevitable by those persons today who treat war as an all-or-nothing state. The Falklands conflict serves as a reminder that this does not have to be so, that limited war employing conventional means (and not even all the conventional means that one side or the other may have available) is a genuine possibility.

Finally, let us return to the question of the proportionality of the war in its *jus ad bellum* sense: was possession of the Falklands worth the price paid? If this is addressed in economic terms alone, the answer must be negative; even before the conflict, the islands were a drain on Britain's economy, and they would have been a drain on Argentina's; after the conflict, the costs must be reckoned much higher. As more than one person has suggested, it would have been cheaper simply to pay the Falklanders to move elsewhere. But economics is not identical with either politics or ethics, and while counting the economic costs must be a part of the total reckoning of proportionality, it is not the only thing to be done. One must also attempt to put such values as national feeling and the need to resist aggression in quantitative terms, for even these are not to be counted as of infinite worth.

The Falklands conflict should become a classic case exemplifying the conduct of limited conventional war between established and similarly armed powers. It also serves as a clear case of the application of just war ideas to the conduct of war, and equally as an example of how these same ideas can be applied to judge contemporary war.

Insurgency-Counterinsurgency Conflict Involving Conventional Weapons: The Israeli War with the PLO

Israel's war with the Palestine Liberation Organization has been a drawn-out and bloody affair marked both by the calculated indiscriminateness of terrorist tactics and the potential for disproportionate destruction of modern weaponry. In this section I will focus on the latter, leaving the subject of terrorism to the following section.

The Israeli–PLO war looked at over its whole history[20] exemplifies a familiar pattern in insurgency–counterinsurgency warfare: the insurgent forces beginning with sabotage and terrorism, while gradually consolidating their political and military strength, over time becoming a de facto government with its own conventional army; opposed by counterinsurgency forces based in an established government, employing force beginning at the level of various forms of police measures and increasingly reliant on conventional military actions. Characteristic of this pattern is that the structure is cumulative and inclusive: the earlier measures are continued along with those begun later, and at any stage in the development of the conflict movement might be toward either end of the scale of possibilities for hostile action.

In the spring of 1982 the PLO was well consolidated politically, and its military forces were better equipped and more numerous than many national armies. Where they were weak (notably in armor and in the air) they could look to other Arab armies for assistance. In Lebanon this meant preeminently to Syrian forces, which had situated themselves in key positions like the Bekaa Valley and were well supplied with both tanks and planes as well as a modern air-defense system. The immediate damage to Israel was coming not from the Syrians, however, who were located well north of the Israeli–Lebanese border, but rather from the shelling of Israeli settlements by PLO artillery. In addition, the PLO continued to employ the tactic of raids against these settlements and against other Israeli population centers, and against Israelis abroad. Israel had itself resorted to countershelling and to raids against the Palestinian population centers from which

PLO forces worked, as well as regularly using surgical air strikes against PLO bases, though often these measures caused considerable collateral harm to noncombatants.

Historically two considerations have produced in the just war tradition a presumption against the legitimacy of insurgency warfare. Accordingly there has come into being a pressure to transform such conflict into the "normative" kind of warfare represented by conventional military clashes between established powers. The first consideration has had to do with the political and military organization of the insurgents, who have until very recently been regarded in the developing tradition as improperly organized rebels or bandits with no legitimate political or military authority. The pressure building out of this consideration, then, has been toward defining the parameters within which an insurgency movement can be treated as having political legitimacy (that is, enjoying right authority or having *compétence de guerre*) and its armed forces as an organized military body rather than a self-seeking, lawless gang of bandits.[21] The PLO had certainly reached the stage of de facto legitimacy by these criteria well before the spring of 1982. The second negative consideration arising out of just war tradition directed against insurgency war has had to do with its methods, which are typically in violation of the *jus in bello* idea that civilian persons going about their peaceful business are noncombatants and not to be the object of hostile actions.[22] But insurgency war depends, in its early stages, on sabotage and terrorism, and these are directed immediately to the noncombatant population. Indeed, in the first stages of an insurgency conflict it would be suicide for the insurgents to attempt a conventional armed clash with counterinsurgency military forces because of the relative disparity in strength. On the other hand it is difficult for conventional military strength to respond appropriately to sabotage and terrorism: when it is applied, such force looks out of proportion to the harm being redressed, and thus the second of the traditional *jus in bello* principles is violated. But counterinsurgency response at the same low level as the initial insurgent activity leads equally to infringements of the rights of noncombatant persons. Thus at this initial level insurgency warfare is intractably dirty, from a moral standpoint. The pressure has accordingly been to transform this sort of war into something more like a conventional military conflict, where the parameters are more manageable and noncombatants are not, at least in principle, to be the object of direct, intentional attack. Politically the transformation of the conflict in this way holds the promise that an end may be in sight if a decisive military victory is won; yet this is dubious, since a military victory might simply result in returning the war to the stage of terrorism and sabotage as the only methods of war employed.

What is instructive in the Israeli–PLO conflict, and in the spring 1982 phase particularly, is the problem of justified means: whether insurgency warfare can measure up to the standards of just war reasoning, and if so in what way. These standards are not highly idealized criteria incapable of attainment in actual conflicts but attempt to be realistic standards by which to judge the conduct of hostilities between enemy parties. What we say here applies directly to the case before us, but by extension it applies to other insurgency conflicts at this stage of development as well. It is in this later stage, when the political and military organization of the insurgents has reached the state of de facto legitimacy and ability to exercise authority that the means of war employed are able to come closest to the moral reference points provided by the ideas of discrimination and proportionality. In the case before us, then, did the means employed in fact represent all that could reasonably have been done in reaching these marks? If not, what else might have been done?

On the PLO side the methods used were mixed and were directed mainly at Israeli noncombatants. This was a clear violation of the principle of noncombatant immunity. The fact that relative PLO weakness meant that the amount of harm inflicted against Israel was lower than that done by the Israelis in return does not affect this judgment on the indiscriminacy of the PLO methods in the war. That is, discrimination takes priority over proportionality in judging the morality of means of war. It was precisely because of their limited military strength relative to the Israelis that the PLO waged a war against Israeli noncombatants. Such war, regardless of mitigating circumstances, is condemned in the moral tradition of just war, and the condemnation is not only moral but a feature of international agreements specifying the law of war.

But another principle in the law of war is reciprocity, which can be taken to imply that if one side violates the immunity of the other's noncombatants, the other side may reciprocate until the initial violation ceases. Morally, however, the shadow over direct, intentional harm to noncombatants remains, requiring that action of the legal right to reciprocity be delayed as long as possible, and then that the acts taken be as restrained as possible while still being efficacious in stopping the indiscriminate acts of the first violators of noncombatant rights. In interstate conflicts enforcement of this right is difficult enough, but the assumption is that harm to noncombatants serves neither the political nor the military ends of war in such a conflict. This was generally regarded as a valid assumption about the conduct of war before World War II, and there are good reasons to think it a valid assumption to govern the fighting of war in any time. If anything, the moral and legal restrictions aimed at protecting noncombatants have grown in recent debate and in international law;[23] yet at the same time it cannot be denied that the practice of war in World War II has produced a certain conviction that war must be unrestrained and that no noncombatant protection is either feasible or desirable. We have seen, though, that in the Falklands war the rights of noncombatants were honored, and we have also seen that one of the arguments in favor of deployment of the neutron warhead is consideration of its lower threat to noncombatants relative to that posed by existing tactical fission weapons. Nonetheless, the lesson of World War II undermining noncombatant protection is hard to forget. If this is the case regarding wars between established powers for traditional aims like territorial claims, then it is far more true of insurgency warfare, where the goal is defined by an ideological commitment that makes an enemy of everyone who does not share that commitment. Such warfare as this, in its disregard of the fundamental rights that follow from noncombatancy, poses a most basic challenge to the possibility of human community.

The principle might be laid down that when a fundamental human value, like the rights of noncombatancy, is threatened, then action may be taken to preserve that value, even if in the short run protecting it may require disregarding it. This is the principle that justifies acts out of supreme emergency, and it is an extremely dangerous one. When invoked, it must be circumscribed by exteme restraint, or else its actions lead directly to what they were meant to correct.

As to the Israeli conduct of their war with the PLO, the erring has in the past been in the direction of disproportionate actions rather than indiscriminacy. The Israelis have intentionally avoided directly attacking noncombatants, though the methods of their war have been of such destructive magnitude that the number of noncombatant casualties has sometimes been high. At least in part the blame is that of the PLO, which sheltered its political and military commands in the midst of residential areas populated by noncombatants. The weapons of modern warfare are especially unsuitable for discriminate use in such environments. Knowing this makes it prudent for insurgency movements to site their bases in this way. But at the same time the fact that doing so is a conscious decision carries with it the burden of responsibility for the noncombatants whose lives are thereby endangered. It is extremely difficult to carry on a war employing restraint, and all the harder when one side is convinced that its aims justify any and all hostile acts. It is extremely difficult to protect noncombatants during a war, and it is all the harder when one side proceeds directly against the other's noncombatants and takes steps that endanger its own. In the face of these considerations, the Israeli actions in its war against the PLO, while not morally without blame, seem to show a pattern of respect for the tradition of restraint in war and protection of the rights of noncombatants that is not even minimally visible among their opponents.

But I suggested earlier that some Israeli acts may have

been disproportionate. What would it mean in this context for an act of war to be proportionate? Applying the paradigm from Augustine with which this book began, we can answer first that even in a justified conflict the defender's primary duty is to protect the innocent. Beyond that, the defender's rights over the attacker extend to restraining him from doing harm, including doing to him whatever he was prepared to do in his attack, but no more. This is the imagery of defensive counterforce warfare, and it is the image at the basis of just war tradition. It may be further drawn out to include restraining the attacker from similar acts in the future and punishing him for the evil he attempted or accomplished before being stopped. While this leads beyond the fundamental imagery of defensive counterforce action, it is not inconsistent with the paradigm, and when Augustine's constraints having to do with intention are added, we have a fairly clear picture of what proportionate warfare is all about. Taking the incursion into Lebanon as our example, we now can ask about its proportionateness as an act in response to the unjust attacks on noncombatants by the PLO.

First, this incursion went considerably beyond defensive counterforce action to include future restraint and punishment. Protecting noncombatants from PLO shelling could have been accomplished by evacuating the endangered settlers beyond the range of the PLO guns. From the Israeli point of view this would not, however, have addressed the problem of protection from terrorist attacks, and it would not have prevented such attacks in the future or punished the previous actions against Israeli noncombatants. Yet it must be suggested that the path of restraint on the part of the Israelis would have been to establish by military means a noncombatant-free area along the border with Lebanon, locating noncombatants out of the reach of PLO artillery and employing electronic detection devices to prevent terrorist infiltration, while continuing the police methods in effect for some time aimed at identifying PLO agents in Israel and apprehending them. Only the first of these options was not taken, being countered by the argument that the

Israeli noncombatants had a right to live within their own borders in peace. Israeli forces have also, though, engaged in punitive actions against the PLO in Lebanon, by means of attacks against the bases of the latter. Though noncombatants have regularly suffered from these attacks along with combatants, the intent was directed against the latter, and as already noted the PLO shares the blame for harm to noncombatants because of their siting of their bases of operation. On this level of action too the Israelis may be judged to have acted within the scope of proportionality, as well as discriminately. But the stage reached in the invasion of Lebanon presents a different picture. Because of the magnitude of the Israeli action large numbers of noncombatants not directly associated with the PLO were affected as well as those already put at risk by close proximity to PLO bases. Long after this particular phase in the war is over the damage done to Lebanese society will endure. Because the effect of such a military action on noncombatants was knowable in advance, we are here at least on the edge of a violation by the Israelis of the principle of noncombatant immunity; yet even if the edge has not been crossed over, the proportionateness of such massive destruction, by comparison with the evils averted, restrained, or punished, would seem to be hard to maintain.[24]

The lessons of this brief look at the Israeli–PLO conflict for insurgency war generally are simple but hard. As already noted, it is extremely difficult for such a war to be waged within the moral boundaries sketched in just war tradition. The pressure has thus arisen to transform insurgency conflict to something more like interstate wars. But until such a transformation is achieved, the difficulty of restraint grows with the conventional military weakness of the warring parties and the degree of ideological fervor present on one or both sides. The essential moral point is that the failure of the insurgents to observe fundamental moral restraints does not absolve the counterinsurgent forces from their duty to do so. Even where protection of noncombatant lives is the ostensible aim, action aimed at insurgent noncombatants is as much a threat to the moral value involved as is the evil committed by the insurgents that it seeks to remedy. Similarly, disproportionately destructive military actions also represent a threat to fundamental human values and are not a proper redress to evils done by the insurgents.

Can insurgency war be just, then? If the methods used involve attacks against fundamental rights like noncombatancy, the answer is no, and this tends to rule out virtually all recent insurgency warfare. High ideological commitment does not excuse such violations. If insurgents are interested in establishing a more moral order, then they must be held to moral means in establishing it. But on the other side the same consideration holds: counterinsurgency may not include violations of the same values that are ostensibly being protected, and the moral order that is being protected must be served by moral means. This may mean that the only effective means of waging insurgency conflicts must be non-military; it certainly suggests that more should be attempted in this direction. Both sides in such a conflict thus must give more attention to political means and make more efforts toward strengthening the society's ability to withstand unjust acts by the other side. In the military sphere both must pay more attention to truly defensive measures and less to retaliatory punishment for evil received.

Terrorism as a Means of War

The canon lawyers who gave legal shape to the developing ideas of the law of war in the Middle Ages absolutely condemned the brigandage they knew as being outside the values of social living. This same condemnation applies to terrorism today. The problem once more hinges on the immunity of noncombatants. Terrorism strikes at the defenseless, not at the combatant forces of a social unit, and is thus by nature a crime against humanity. Michael Walzer has suggested that the line of distinction between combatants and noncombatants might be redrawn so as to include political officials in the former category, thus making them legitimate targets for insurgent movements.[25] That some (though not all) political officials are combatants in a war is an old idea in just war tradition, but in any case to make such an observation does not strike at the heart of the problem posed by terrorism, which is that this form of force aims directly at noncombatants, attempting by creating fear among the defenseless to undermine the political structures that are supposed to provide protection.

I am, of course, speaking here first of all about insurgency terrorism, though counterinsurgency use of terrorist methods is equally to be condemned. In either case it is the direct, intentional violence against the innocent that marks this form of the use of force as fundamentally evil. Yet other moral problems surround terrorism as well, and their root might well be put in the words of a French peasant quoted in a sixteenth-century book on the horrors of the wars of religion in France: "Who will believe that your cause is just," the peasant queries, "when your behaviors are so unjust?"[26] This question must be posed to all modern war, but it poses a particular challenge to terrorism. For the claim is typically advanced that the overwhelming justice of the cause justifies the kinds of actions terrorists commit. This claim must be examined to see what it is worth, and the answer is that it is worth nothing.

First, the idea of just cause must be tested by the presence of the other traditional ideas that together determine when resort to force is justified. In particular we need to raise to view three objections: (a) A claim to justice that is fundamentally ideological is not a sufficient justification for the use of force because such claims are not subject to verification. This was the problem posed in the sixteenth-century wars of religion: there is simply no way to decide for one religious faith over another in terms of its justness as a source for moral and political behavior. In working through this problem and rejecting religion as just cause for war, Western moral tradition on war implicitly rejected all such recourse to unverifiable truth claims.[27] The assertion that one's cause is right in some metaphysical sense is not enough to justify violence. (b) The claim to have just cause rests on the presence of an authority able to determine when an injustice is present affecting the community of persons for whom the authority acts, and the authority must be in fact derived from the support of those persons as well as the asserted intent to act on their behalf.[28] This problem of right authority is especially critical in the case of terrorism because whether it is insurgency or counterinsurgency terrorist activity that is at stake, the nature of such activity leads to its being practiced by relatively small cadres of people, cut off personally (and often politically) from the community on whose behalf they claim to operate. (c) It is difficult or impossible to judge that terrorism represents the kinds of attitudes that, in just war tradition, define right intent in the use of force. Rather we seem to have in terrorism precisely a "desire for harming," a "cruelty of avenging," an "implacable animosity," a "lust for domination." In short, it is incoherent to claim just cause when it cannot be verified, there is no evidence of popular support, and there is every evidence of a wrong intention in the use of violence.

But further, the claim that the justice of a terrorist's cause legitimizes harming the innocent must be tested from the standpoint of what is morally allowable in the use of force. This claim is that the end justifies the means, and for just war tradition this is very simply not true. The value of the end sought may, certainly, help to determine the means used via the principle of proportionality. In its *jus ad bellum* sense, proportionality has to do with the calculation of total good vs. evil done in connection with the conflict at issue, and in this sense of the term a greater evil to be remedied or good to be achieved can justify a higher level of destruction. But in its *jus in bello* sense proportionality refers to the adjustment of levels of force and types of force to the problem at hand, as well as to the application of force in a counterforce, defensive way. Only in the former sense does the claim that terrorist tactics are justified by a supremely good cause have any merit to it, and this merit is immediately dissolved by the inconsistency between such tactics and the meaning of proportionality in its *jus in bello* sense. Further, sharp divergence between terrorism and the implications of the principle of discrimination has already been noted as the most fundamental problem with terrorism; nothing in the cause could modify this.

Thus in terrorism we have, at the opposite end of the spectrum I have sketched from strategic nuclear war, a form of contemporary armed conflict that is equally evil, and for the same basic reasons: the incommensurability between the values served and the destruction of values created, and the fact that both rely on threats to noncombatants as their basic means of procedure. Between these two extremes are three types of contemporary war that may or may not be justified according to circumstances, but that in principle are morally possible means of applying force in the service of endangered human values. The discussion in this chapter provides an overview or orientation to the principal kinds of armed conflict that characterize our present stage in history. Subsequent chapters, particularly those in parts III and IV below, will treat many of the issues raised here in greater breadth and detail. The lessons of the present chapter, though, are two: that while some kinds of modern war are morally possible, it takes work to make the use of military force in fact stay within the boundaries of our principal moral tradition of justification and restraint in war; and that every effort should be made to eliminate reliance on two forms of contemporary use of force, strategic nuclear weapons and terrorism, as inherently at odds with the values expressed in this moral tradition.

II

Contemporary Weapons

3

Morally Legitimate Defense

Introduction

For a generation United States defense posture has heavily
rested, in one form or another, on the possession of a strategic nuclear deterrent force targeted principally or wholly
on the Soviet Union. In varying proportions over time, but
always as a component in the strategy of deterrence, the
specific targets have included population centers rather than
military installations as such. At the same time the United
States has maintained, at various levels at various times, a
conventional military capacity of its own and has entered
into alliances aimed at expanding that latter capacity. The
degree to which our alliances (NATO is the chief example)
have increased the effectiveness of the nuclear deterrent can
be debated, but what is not debatable is that the United
States has regularly and consistently sought to involve other
nations in regional or global schemes to deter the outbreak
of a major war and to cooperate in fighting such a war
should it come.[1] Whatever the moral deficiencies of a nuclear deterrent policy that threatens (whether explicitly or
implicitly) large numbers of noncombatants with death, suffering over a short or long term, and loss of livelihood for the
survivors, the proponents of this policy, as we noted in the

last chapter, have been quick to point out that it has worked: there has been no nuclear holocaust; a nuclear weapon has never been fired except for test purposes since Hiroshima and Nagasaki.[2] And even moralists have been of two minds on the matter, as suggested by the guarded and limited "toleration" of deterrence expressed in the recent pastoral letter of the American Catholic bishops.[3] Nonetheless, so far as the nuclear deterrent element of United States defense policy is concerned, an enormous risk clearly exists that some event, whether accidental or designed, will produce a massive nuclear interchange between the West and the East. Should this occur, it will be little comfort indeed for critics to note that the deterrent proved to be ineffective, that the fact that these strategic arsenals were used shows the whole policy to have been a grand mistake.

Yet it is no small part of the nuclear dilemma that the transition from strategic deterrence policy to some other form of defense structure is fraught with peril. Whenever any attempt has been made toward such a transition away from a massive counterpopulation threat as our principal strategy, critics have been quick to attack it as a threat to international stability. This was true when tactical nuclear arms were introduced into Europe; it was true also later on when two secretaries of defense, MacNamara and then Schlesinger, announced their versions of counterforce strategic targeting as a move away from such heavy reliance on counterpopulation targeting, and still later when the neutron bomb was first proposed for development, and most recently when Presidential Directive 59 was issued, explicitly associating the Carter administration with the idea of counterforce strategy. There is no small irony in the fact that some of the opponents of counterpopulation strategy on moral grounds have been vocally opposed to efforts to transform our national defense posture away from this strategy, alleging the creation of instability.

In the case of military matters the relevant moral tradition from our general cultural past overlaps significantly the relevant moral tradition from our religious heritage. I use the term *just war tradition* for both because they are inextricably intertwined. The wisdom of this joint tradition may be stated simply, using the terms Paul Ramsey employed[4] to describe the attitude on war of St. Augustine of Hippo: permission, yet limitation. There are times when to protect the highest values of the civilization, war may become necessary. Yet in the protection of those values there must be a pervasive effort to limit and restrain the harm that may be done. Some actions may never be allowable; others must be subjected to the test of whether the evil they cause may be greater than the good they do. Ramsey connected these twin themes, permission with limitation, to Augustine and thus specifically Christian tradition on war; yet, as I have tried to demonstrate in my writings,[5] they characterize Western cultural thought on war generally. The moralist speaking in the public forum, then, bears the obligation to clarify what values of our culture are worth protecting at what cost, and he or she bears the equally heavy responsibility to seek to define what restraint or limitation may mean in the contemporary context.

Following are several assertions or propositions about what morally legitimate defense would involve. The interpretation and justification of these statements will define the argument of this chapter.

1. Noncombatants should be protected from the ravages of war, and a defense policy specifically oriented around harm or a threat to harm noncombatants is morally wanting.
2. Armaments should be judged morally not in terms of whether or not they are nuclear but rather in terms of their intended use in war.
3. A moral defense strategy should aim at the development of weapons of defense and offense that may be morally employed if need should arise.
4. A defense strategy should be flexible and thus should incorporate potential responses to aggression at every conceivable level from a simple military presence up to and including all-out war. This implies a much heavier reliance on conventional forces than we now have.
5. A moral defense strategy for the United States should involve resumption of the military draft.

1. Noncombatants should be protected from the ravages of war.

Underlying everything that I will say about the structure of morally legitimate defense is a conviction that restraint or limitation of harm done is a chief moral goal to be served in military planning. This has in fact been one of the overriding first principles of Western moral thought on war throughout its history.[6] So far as the limitation of war once begun is concerned (the *jus in bello*) the principal focus has been on the limitation of harm to noncombatants, though there have also been other themes.

Several of these deserve mention. One has been to attempt to limit weapons, and I will treat that in the following chapter. Another, tried and found wanting in the Middle Ages, was to attempt to limit the days in which armies could fight: generally, they had to avoid religious holidays. We have the residue of that conception still with us in Christmas truces, Tet truces, and so on, but the regular breakdown of such ceasefires in the Vietnam war, not to mention in the Yom Kippur war between Arabs and Israelis, should remind us of the difficulties of this approach to restraint. Generally speaking, such truces do not work at all in conflicts between substantially different cultures, and they have had a poor history even in wars between belligerents with similar cultures. Still another effort at restraint has focused on harm to the combatant; probably the classic instance of this kind is the Hague Law provision against unlimited means of injuring the enemy, mentioning specifically poison as a weapon and "arms, projectiles, or material of a nature to cause superfluous injury"[7] Such provisions in international law aim directly at protecting the combatant while he is yet a combatant; moral discussion, as well as other approaches in international law,[8] has tended to consider also those injuries to the combatant that have a persistent or lingering effect after the war has ended, when all former combatants have become noncombatants. To my knowledge John Locke was the first theorist to take this problem of lingering injury at all seriously,[9] but if it is pursued, the result is that weapons whose effect is inevitably to cause long-term damage, including for example defoliants and other chemical weapons as well as radiation weapons, are called in question. (Obviously some such effects follow from all weapons of war, and so a decision must be made; the moral rule of double effect needs to be applied seriously to such cases. But my point is that some classes of weapons are much worse than others in this regard.) The rule of double effect has been employed to justify collateral noncombatant casualties from an air strike whose intent was to demolish a legitimate military target.[10] Leaving aside the whole question of whether surgical air strikes in war conditions can in fact closely discriminate between legitimate targets and nearby or otherwise available illegitimate ones, it seems to me reasonable to argue that the double effect rule is wrongly applied to the use of weapons which are demonstrably broadly destructive or incapable of consistent discriminating use even under the best of conditions. Heavy megatonnage nuclear and thermonuclear weapons fall into the first category, while chemical and bacteriological weapons fall into the latter. When the long-term destructive effects of such weapons are added to the considerations of immediate possibility of discriminating use, the moral case against them becomes worse. If the traditional moral wisdom is to be honored, that noncombatants should so far as possible be spared the ravages of war, then the implication seems clear: the use of such weapons as these now available should be avoided wherever possible and restrained if avoidance is impossible; and development of new weapons should be concentrated on types of systems whose known effects will render them more capable of discriminating use and will be immediate rather than persistent over a long term.

This leads finally to the broader issue of the protection of noncombatants generally. What has been said above might be repeated here. The issue is a real one, for practical limits set on harm to noncombatants in previous ages have all but evaporated in our own time, leaving only intentional limits, those applied as a result of a conscious decision.[11] Those earlier practical limits may be summarized as set by the nature of armies, the nature of states, and the nature of the means of war.

When armies were relatively small, composed of a professional or quasi-professional class of men, it was relatively easy to determine who was a combatant and who a noncombatant, so as to be able to treat the latter differently from the former. The rise of national armies and the *levée en masse* during the Napoleonic period is usually cited as the death blow to the small professional army, though the shift toward the national army began as early as the sixteenth century.[12] Along with this sea change must be counted the transformation in the nature of national states so that wars were no longer a matter of disputes among rulers but rather a matter of protecting or extending the way of life of a whole people. Again, the wars of the French Revolution and the Napoleonic period exemplify this change. Finally there is what Michael Mandelbaum has called the "mechanical revolution" in warfare, the application of the industrial age to weapons, logistics, and mobilization.[13] This transformation began to change warfare definitively in the 1860s and 1870s and is still under way, though the age of nuclear arms has brought another sweeping change. If we are, as some observers believe, on the verge of yet another revolution, this time an electronic and cybernetic one, then elements from these earlier decisive changes will be shaped further.

Once again, the point is that each stage in the modern and contemporary transformation of warfare has removed some of the internal and necessary constraints that previously held the destructiveness of war in check. It is relatively easy to observe how much earlier ages depended on those internal constraints. Two examples, widely separated in time and circumstance, will illustrate this. First, consider the medieval consensus on noncombatant immunity, which can be summarized in the statement that all persons should be considered noncombatants who, because of infirmity, age, or sex, were unable to bear arms, as well as (under normal conditions) all persons not of the knightly class. The prevalent practice of siege warfare in this period meant that indirect harm to noncombatants could not be avoided, and the need for knights and their retainers to live off the land while on the march tended also to prevent full compliance with this ideal; yet chivalric considerations pointed toward battle only with worthy enemies, and the limited means of force available in medieval armies meant that this force could not be squandered in militarily unproductive pillaging of peasants on the land and travelers on the roads. The classes of persons named as noncombatants were also not normally involved in battles between medieval armies in the field, such as at Crécy and Agincourt. The circumstances of medieval warfare thus made noncombatant immunity, as understood in the terms of that time, relatively easy to grant.[14]

Second, consider the kind of noncombatant protection achieved in the limited wars of the eighteenth century, where the majority of the populace in a nation at war might never see a hostile soldier. Warfare was conducted chiefly by maneuver aimed at securing strategic spots—"magazines," or fortified military depots, mountain passes, richly productive areas. While this era saw no particular attempt to protect noncombatants inside strategic areas of maneuver, the point of such warfare included the protection of everyone else; there was no reason to win a war only to have a devastated nation on one's hands. Hence the populace outside the theater of war enjoyed an almost absolute protection.[15] Now, an important common denominator of these two examples is the geographic factor: remoteness from combat for most noncombatants supported noncombatant immunity as an ideal. With the disappearance of this geographic factor and of other built-in limitations in warfare of earlier periods, only the ideal remains, and it must be achieved through intentionality only or principally.

2. Armaments should be judged morally not in terms of whether or not they are nuclear but rather in terms of their intended use in war.

In the previous section we began to address the issue of how armaments should be judged morally, for discussing the protection of noncombatants requires some discussion of the means of warfare. In examining this proposition more closely, we must begin by recognizing that from a moral standpoint rooted in the Western tradition of restraint in

war there is undoubtedly much wrong with nuclear weaponry in the forms and projected uses it has had since 1945.

1. Nuclear bombs and missiles have been designed to be as powerful
   as possible so that discrimination between legitimate and illegitimate targets in practice is in most cases not a real possibility.
2. Except in some versions of limited response doctrine, the targets
   of the strategic nuclear force are population centers, not military
   installations, thus withdrawing the possibility of discrimination
   through intention.
3. Depending on the level at which a warhead is detonated, it may
   be relatively "dirty" or "clean" in its radiation effects, but in
   any case a persistent residue of radiation effect would remain
   after detonation to continue to menace the living after the end of
   a nuclear war.
4. The effect of nuclear war on the total environment of the earth
   has been variously estimated, both positively and negatively,
   but certainly represents some level of risk not comparable to
   that from previous (non-nuclear) wars.

These caveats apply chiefly to strategic weapons, which
make up the majority of the nuclear arsenal, but similar
observations may be made about the tactical nuclear weapons now deployed. It is especially true that, since they have
been fission weapons and not fusion, the relative "dirtiness"
of tactical weapons is high. Also, in spite of the battlefield
designation of use of such weapons, the most likely theater
for their employment remains Western Europe, where the
effect of a high population density negates the effect of the
low megatonnage of tactical nuclear warheads. It would be
impossible to fight a war in this area using tactical nuclear
weapons without considerable harm to noncombatants from
these weapons, and thus the problem of discrimination here
turns out to be similar to that in the case of strategic weaponry. Finally in this connection there exists an admitted risk
of escalation from tactical to strategic nuclear interchange,
if only for the reason that under battlefield conditions any
nuclear blast may look much like any other.
But much pertaining to these difficulties with nuclear
weapons also applies to other contemporary means of war.
Surely chemical and biological weapons, as already noted,

carry with their use the problems of potential overkill, indiscriminateness, and residual effects both known and unknown. Even so-called conventional weapons have progressed in destructive capability to the point that they too may cause staggering losses in human lives, livelihoods, and property, and undoubtedly too some of their effects are residual, affecting noncombatants after a war as well as during it. A classic and still relevant example is the air war of World War II, which caused more destruction with conventional bombs than was effected at Hiroshima and Nagasaki, and whose long-term effects have been at least comparable to those of the two atomic bombs used in that war.

So, in short, the problem is not nuclear weapons as such. Rather it is a mixture of the destructive potential of modern weapons, whether nuclear, bacteriological, chemical, or conventional, with an intentionality for use of those weapons that envisions war as a kind of holocaust.[16] And it is this component of intentionality that, I suggest, deserves more careful ethical analysis.

3. A moral defense strategy should aim at the development of weapons of defense and offense that may be morally employed if need should arise.

Just war tradition envisions some conflicts that are justified and some means of engaging in justified conflicts that are themselves justified. Much opposition to modern war has centered on the impossibility of justifying such war because of the disproportionate (hence immoral) destructiveness of available weapons. Another line of attack, as already noted, has centered on their indiscriminateness.[17] By this reasoning, while there may have been a possibility of just warfare in the past, modern weapons remove that possibility. Such weapons do not have to be nuclear (though this is a familiar argument among opponents of nuclear weaponry); the arguments from proportion and discrimination were both leveled against the Vietnam war, in which only conventional weapons were employed. In the development of just war tradition this represents a new turn: the employment of *jus in bello* reasoning to determine the absence of a *jus ad bellum*.

One mode of response to this kind of criticism of modern warfare has been the development of limited war doctrine. Such doctrine has been advanced in several forms and combinations of forms: limitation by geographical region, by the objectives or ends sought, by the weapons used, and by the targets chosen.[18] The first, second, and last of these modes of limitation correlate directly with the limited warfare of the eighteenth century, probably the best historical example of such limitation of conflict, though in that warfare the weapons were self-limiting. Interestingly, such notably fierce contemporary conflicts as the Vietnam and Yom Kippur wars were limited warfare by all four criteria; this suggests that the answers given in limited war doctrine do not go far enough to satisfy many who object to modern war on *jus in bello* grounds. But a contrary case can also be argued: that under present conditions such modes of limitation represent the best possible moral answer to the necessity of fighting in a war, once it has been determined that the war itself is justified. This latter argument puts the stress on the *jus ad bellum* over the *jus in bello*, which is where it has traditionally lain. But in the past, it might be retorted, weapons were less destructive and more discriminate; it is the new conditions which necessitate placing *jus in bello* considerations first.

How may this argument be resolved, if it may? I myself am not at all convinced by the *jus in bello* argument against the possibility of justifying *any* modern warfare. When Franciscus de Victoria, the Spanish neo-scholastic who more than any other individual served to recast the medieval just war consensus for the dawning of the modern age, approached the problem of proportion and discrimination in warfare, he in the end subordinated them to considerations of the rightness of waging war in the first place. His position is representative of the whole sweep of the tradition—at least up to the last century or so of opposition to war. The context in which his argument was developed was an analysis of siege warfare.[19] When attacking a besieged city in a war known to be just, Victoria reasoned, an army may use indiscriminate weapons like cannon and fire even though clearly noncombatants may be hurt along with combatants. Similarly, in the storming of such a city the attacking forces are not to be held guilty for damage done to civilian lives and property (though good discipline and the ends of war—prominent nonmoral factors in Victoria's analysis—served as restraints on such harm).

But what Victoria said here about the primacy of *jus ad bellum* over *jus in bello* must also be read in conjunction with what I have called his doctrine of simultaneous ostensible justice.[20] This is the idea that in most conflicts, because of the complex nature of the causes for which the war might be fought, lack of clarity about the ratio of total good to total evil a war might effect, and conflicting lines of authority to make war, both sides may, as far as they can possibly know, be acting justly. Rather than saying that both may then use every means of warfare possible to them, Victoria argues that they must both then use restraint in waging the war. This too becomes representative of the just war tradition.

When these two somewhat contradictory positions are placed alongside each other, two implications appear. One direction of reasoning, which I will not pursue here, points in the direction of the position identified by Michael Walzer as the argument from supreme emergency.[21] Stated in basic form, this is the argument that while restraint may be appropriate in war under most conditions, when the fundamental values of a nation or civilization are threatened, then a case of supreme emergency exists that justifies the most total means available. Proceeding the other way, we encounter a moral imperative to develop effective means of war that may be used proportionately and with discrimination, so effective that the necessity of using totalistic means may never arise.[22] This is the point I wish to pursue in the present connection, leaving the former to be discussed in chapter 8 below.

The point may be put in this way: If it is accepted that some value or values exist whose protection may require use of military force—whatever that value or values may be—then the moral reasoning of the *jus in bello* in just war tradition requires that means be created suitable to that end. If the means available to protect these values are only ones which, if used, contravene the values themselves—the case Walzer considers under the supreme emergency rubric—then not enough has been done, morally speaking, to follow through the implication of having values worth protecting by forceful means. To argue against the strategic nuclear arsenal without making clear what alternative should replace it amounts to either a mistaken logic or a denial that any values this culture has are worth preserving by war. If the latter is the case, then nuclear pacifism and absolute pacifism are not so different after all. But if the former is the case, then the implication of creating means suitable to the desired ends must be followed through. If we are not to have a war employing strategic nuclear weapons, then alternative weapons systems must be developed that will effectively replace such weapons. This, I believe, is the real key to nuclear disarmament. Because such disarmament is a hotly debated issue, I will comment briefly on this link before returning to the issue of effective, rational, and morally acceptable means of defense.

In his recent book *The Nuclear Revolution* Michael Mandelbaum develops an extended comparison between nuclear and chemical weapons in order to examine why the latter have proved susceptible to limitation by treaty and other means, while the former have generally not. In general, his conclusion is that the effectiveness of efforts at arms limitation is in inverse proportion to the usefulness and reliability of the weapons being limited.[23] I am convinced of the rightness of this reasoning and develop a similar case in the following chapter. Historical analysis reveals that weapons bans have never been more than a minor strain in Western cultural tradition on the restraint of war, and this for two reasons: first, such bans illegitimately turn the focus of moral analysis toward specific weapons and away from the moral agent who may choose to use or not use them; and second, in practice it has been lack of military utility that has been decisive in those few weapons bans that have proven effective. As an illustration, consider that while nuclear arms limits or outright banning have been no more workable than the medieval attempt to ban crossbows and siege engines, a taboo on the use of poison has persisted throughout Western tradition on war. The paradigmatic case is the poisoning of water supplies. What appears in the literature to be wrong with this is that once the poison is in place, no one can really control where it goes, who ingests it, what effect it may have, or how long that effect may last. Chemical weapons share these defects. Surely, though, nuclear weapons do as well. In his analysis of this issue Mandelbaum addresses this last point, arguing that the closeness of the analogy with poison as a weapon is obscured in the case of nuclear weapons because their level of development has given them a kind of utility that poison in a well or gas on the battlefield could never have. In a nutshell, he argues that what happened is that the blast effect of nuclear weapons—that which makes them predictable and controllable and thus like conventional weapons—has overridden the poison effect—the wide-ranging, persistent, and poisonous radiation damage.

The conclusion of all this reasoning, much compressed in the above brief account, is that an effective ban on nuclear weapons is likely to be possible only after replacements have been found that limit their utility and/or surpass them in the effects desired. Because of the serious moral problems inherent in reliance on a counterpopulation strategic deterrent as the main line of defense, the energies of moral criticism need to be focused strongly on what might replace such reliance. The replacements should be designed so that they can be more readily employed in accord with the moral traditions of our culture. This means that they must be proportionate to the ends of war and for use against combatant forces rather than noncombatants; yet they must also be effective enough in protecting the highest values of our culture that no argument from supreme emergency can successfully interject disproportionate and nondiscriminating methods of war.

So we are speaking of counterforce weapons as the mainline of our defense reliance, but we are stipulating that such weapons should be of the highest order of effectiveness both to deter war and to protect our highest values should war come.

The two paths to the goals I have sketched, limiting the effectiveness of strategic nuclear weapons and meeting or surpassing them in the production of desirable effects (the corollary of which is the production of fewer negative effects), are, respectively, the paths of defense and of offense, in the proper meanings of these terms; they might be called, in the nomenclature of another day, the shield and the sword. I will discuss both of these approaches further in later chapters.

4. A defense strategy should be flexible and thus should incorporate potential responses to aggression at every conceivable level from a simple military presence up to and including all-out war. This implies a much heavier reliance on conventional forces than we now have.

Once the idea is accepted that it is sometimes justifiable to use force to oppose the actions of another state, we are in the realm of just war tradition. We are also in the realm of the real world, in which national values compete with one another by all sorts of means, the use of force being one of them. Apart from the question of how to decide that a given action should be opposed by military means, which is a political and legal question as well as a moral one, there is the question of what sort of force to employ. Here we encounter at its fullest the requisite that has endured throughout the history of development of the just war tradition that the use of force be proportionate to the evil under way. There is a *jus ad bellum* version of this question, pointing to the need to count the total costs of a war, so far as they can be known in advance, before pronouncing that entry into it justified, and there is also a *jus in bello* version, in which attention is directed to opposing effectively the particular threat that is imminent or already in process. While I am here thinking principally in the latter mode, the implications of the *jus ad bellum* consideration of proportionality point in the same direction. That direction leads us to doctrines of limited warfare and flexible response, and beyond them to the means of warfare appropriate to those ends. A variety of types of conventional forces, trained and equipped and kept at a level of readiness suitable to their respective missions, turns out to represent the closest approach to appropriate means of war available in our present context.

It is symptomatic of the American approach to military affairs in the nuclear age that we have sought in many cases systematically to substitute nuclear weaponry for manpower. Nuclear weaponry indeed offers some genuine advantages of cost-effectiveness over conventional forces. But these advantages come at the expense of the very values military preparedness is supposed to protect—values which are substantially linked to the centuries-old moral tradition teaching us to seek to protect noncombatants from the ravages of war. A further disadvantage is the danger of escalation, about which nothing more needs to be said here. Still further, even the smallest nuclear warheads (those of the tactical variety, including the neutron bomb) are too large for proportionate use except against fairly large targets. Under wartime conditions a simple misreading of an enemy threat or a conscientious desire to get a job done even at the cost of some overkill could lead a commander to choose such disproportionately destructive weapons. I consider this a very real possibility, inasmuch as it represents a straightforward extension of principles and practices familiar to anyone with command responsibility: save the soldiers under your command by using firepower where possible. Under the conditions of modern war this has led to huge levels of destructiveness in the name of a rationally perceived military necessity. Yet the idea of proportionality in just war tradition clearly points in the opposite direction: toward matching of weapons to enemy threats and behavior at every level. The only way to reconcile these two opposing tendencies is to prepare military forces that are genuinely effective at every level of hostility. This implies undergirding nuclear armaments by a network of conventional military capability so structured as to render the need for disproportionate actions—including the use of nuclear weaponry—less and less compelling. That strong conventional forces can substitute for nuclear weapons seems so obvious as not to require stating. But United States military preparedness has in the past, for admittedly attractive economic and political reasons, moved in exactly the opposite direction. The question thus is whether the moral reasons—those rooted in the ideas of proportion and protection of noncombatants—should not outweigh the political and economic ones.[24]

This brings us to the matter of how to create and sustain a military with a considerably larger personnel component than is present today without producing overwhelming economic and political burdens on our society.

5. A moral defense strategy for the United States should involve resumption of the military draft.

The idea that the burden of national defense should be borne by all citizens is as old as the two main sources of Western culture, ancient Greece and biblical Israel. In the modern period this idea has taken on only a new form, as in the thought of Rousseau. And after the Napoleonic revolution in the composition of armies the draft became a regular feature of national life in continental Europe. In the so-called Anglo-Saxon countries, though—Britain and the United States—conscription has generally been associated with the actual fighting of wars rather than with military preparedness during peacetime. United States practice after World War II, maintaining the military draft right up to the end of the conflict in Vietnam, represents an exception to this generality. What is perhaps remarkable is that during the thirty-odd years of this "peacetime" conscription, the obligation it represented, the citizen's responsibility to share in the military defense of the nation, was so universally accepted.

Only in the wake of the Vietnam conflict, a broadly unpopular war, did the consensus as to this responsibility disintegrate. The reasons for its disintegration are perhaps myriad, but I suggest two as among the most important. First, American involvement in the Vietnam conflict was widely perceived, in spite of repeated iteration of the domino theory, as not necessary to our national defense. This undermined the willingness of male citizens of draft age to accept service in this war as one of their responsibilities of citizenship. Second, the concept of selective service, worthwhile in itself, under the conditions of the Vietnam conflict led to a draft that was easy to avoid by those inclined to do so. The result was a perception that the draft, rather than being a means of sharing the military burden equitably among all Americans, was instead a legally fraudulent means of enlisting the poor, the uneducated, and the nonwhite while those at the other end of the socioeconomic scale could utilize loopholes in the rules of selective service so as to take their ease as civilians.

Any resumption of military conscription today would have to deal with these two objections. The first one reminds us that the citizen's responsibility in a democratic state is national defense, and that a conscripted military in a democracy simply *may not be able to be used* in ways that are not obviously connected to this end. Two implications flow from this: that dependence on a conscripted national defense force may deter possible political adventurism on the part of U.S. leaders that might lead to war, and, pointing in the opposite direction, that a substantial portion of the available military force should be composed of volunteer professionals who can be used for purposes integral to national defense but not such as to require the political and ideological mobilization of the entire nation. These two opposing implications provide checks on each other: against misuse of conscripted forces and against the necessity of making each military conflict, however great or minor and however closely or remotely connected to national defense, a so-called holy war. Had we as a people thought through these implications seriously in the Vietnam case, this country might not have become involved in that conflict in the way we did, or we might alternatively have matched a deep involvement with consensual national support. In either case, that divisive episode in our history might have been averted.

The second objection mentioned above, that the draft during the period of the Vietnam conflict was racially, economically, and educationally discriminatory, also requires serious treatment. I am convinced that when a conscripted military is being properly employed such a perception of discrimination is not likely to arise. In any case the problem is not the idea of selective service, which represents a rational and moral way of allocating the responsibilities of citizenship. But unfortunately the political costs of this idea are extremely high when the total number of personnel needed is relatively small as compared to the pool of persons available. Selective service, conscription by lot, and universal conscription are all, as such, moral means to the end of sharing the burdens of citizenship. In spite of a contemporary fascination among professional ethicists for the use of a lottery in difficult cases,[25] I remain unconvinced that the lottery offers the best way to deal with this problem. Nonetheless, the solution to the problem is necessarily a political one, and the role of the moralist is only advisory. In that advisory capacity my own preference is for a renewed version of selective service rather than either of the other alternatives, but a selective service broadly enough conceived to avoid in practice the kinds of discrimination that occurred during the period of the Vietnam war. So conceived, the resulting military would be more closely representative of the nation's citizenry than is the case with the volunteer military today—which is disproportionately composed of the poor, the poorly educated, and the nonwhite.

Conclusion

This analysis has attempted to move from insights characteristic of Western moral tradition on the restraint of war to some implications of those insights for United States military posture in the next two decades. A great deal more might be said. I have, for example, for the most part avoided the matter of the *jus ad bellum*—whether it is justified in a particular instance to resort to military force. I have in this discussion simply assumed that as in all past ages of human life on this planet there continue to exist values worth fighting for, even in the face of grave dangers. But as I hope I have made plain above, to take this possibility seriously within the context provided by our dominant moral tradition means thinking about war and the weapons of war in a significantly different way from what has been generally practiced in the nuclear age. In short, if the potential or actual use of military force is to be envisioned as a moral possibility, then it behooves us to design that force so that it can be used morally. The first requisite of moral use is human control, and I am utterly unsympathetic to the argument that advances in weaponry are such that human control in time of actual war is unthinkable. If the possibility of human control is unthinkable in fact, it is because of our decision to make it so, not because of something inherent in the weapons themselves. Indeed, in one fundamental sense the availability of weapons of mass destruction makes possible for the first time war as a truly moral activity—that is, one whose limits are determined by human choice rather than by the weapons used. But this possibility carries with it a responsibility—the responsibility to be ready to impose limits on what will be done instead of simply accepting what can be done. Thus I have argued that our nation should be developing strategies of defense and of combat designed not to put noncombatants at risk but rather to protect them, and designed not to produce Armageddon but rather to be effective deterrents and responses across a broad scale of threats to our values. These policy goals, I have further argued, should give direction to our weapons research and development. Both of these thrusts lead away from reliance on counterpopulation threats as the keystone of American defense policy and away from dependence on nuclear weaponry at the expense of military preparedness based on other kinds of force.

In all that I have been saying I have wished to make clear that it is not the weapons of war in our time but the assumptions about war that are most morally questionable. Weapons are but tools of human intentions, and the reason we now live in a world where entire populations are threatened by nuclear missiles is that we have come to regard such threats as appropriate. I will return to this theme in chapters 5 and 6 below.

4

Weapons Limits and the Restraint of War: A Just War Critique

The just war tradition, as we have seen earlier, may be thought of in a variety of ways, but for the purposes of this chapter these may be condensed into two. First, conceived as a moral doctrine, its function is to provide a basis from which to judge actual and proposed weapons and weapons systems and to prepare the conceptual and attitudinal groundwork out of which more moral weapons may arise. Second, conceived as a statement of a cultural consensus, in the form of a more or less coherent though broadly based set of traditional restraints on the resort to war and the conduct of war, just war tradition may be employed to test the continuity between the way we think about such matters today and the ways people linked to us by ties of historical continuity thought about them in the past. These two meanings of just war tradition overlap, and in particular the second should serve as a reminder that the first, the application of moral principles to contemporary cases, must necessarily be undertaken with an eye always focused on the historical developments that have brought to consciousness the moral values encapsulated in those principles.

Arms control, the subject on which this chapter's critique is focused, may also be defined in a variety of ways. It may be used to refer to the attempt to abolish war; more properly it refers to limits of some sort on certain weapons or all weapons. International law contains a number of such restrictions, and as I understand it, this makes them a part of just war tradition. But still it makes sense to distinguish between those limits on weapons that more closely reflect the historical values of this tradition, according to which not particular weapons themselves but certain uses of *any* available weapons are restrained by the ideas of noncombatant immunity and proportional reaction to wrong done, and those other sorts of limits, most of them of relatively recent vintage, which focus upon specific weapons or types of weapons as *mala in se*. The meanings that are attached to the term *arms control* tend to vary according to the perspective—whether military, political, legal, moral, or some other—of the person using the term. Much of the time debate over arms control—or in the other phrases I have used, weapons limits or restrictions—represents a mixture of these various perspectives. So does just war tradition, and I would simply have us be aware of that. Only in the contemporary era has the difference among these various points of view come to matter much for the sake of analysis; farther back in history they are inevitably mixed. Though I will not discuss it further in this chapter, methodologically I believe it better to undertake a just war analysis by attempting to understand the nature and effects of such mixtures. Here I will simply assume for the sake of the present analysis that the various perspectives relate to one another, and in particular that there is a moral component even in considerations of a primarily military or political nature.

It remains to say why just war tradition provides a fitting base from which to conduct an analysis of attempts at restrictions on the weapons of war. A general answer may be given in terms of the two senses of just war tradition defined at the beginning of this chapter. First, as a moral doctrine the just war idea provides a far richer, more finely focused, and in a word more adequate basis for undertaking such analysis than other moral analytical bases. The principles through which just war doctrine expresses itself are historically and thematically linked to fundamental religious and secular moral values; they demonstrably express a wide-spread cultural consensus on the appropriate uses and limits of violence; and they have stood the test of time.[1] By contrast the most outstanding alternative value bases are not nearly so useful. The utilitarianism of most recent philosophical discussion of morality in war is at once too thin and too narrow and, in just war perspective, appears at its best to represent a kind of attempt to reinvent the wheel.[2] The unfocused appeal to humanity often made in twentieth-century international law and likewise made with some frequency by antiwar activists not only is too blurry in its meaning to be useful but also appears to rest on other, more basic, moral principles that are left unacknowledged and unexamined.[3] Finally, the value base offered by pacifism points logically at the absolute banning of all weapons and so is relatively less suited to proximate, relative judgments among weapons; further, overall it appears better suited to an analysis of the eschatological era than of sinful human history, where war and weapons of war remain a fact of life.[4]

In the second sense of just war tradition defined earlier, it is appropriate to undertake an analysis of efforts at weapons restraint in terms of just war ideas because those attempts themselves lie in some relationship with the overall tradition of limits on war denominated the just war tradition. In this connection, the purpose of such analysis is to make clear the nature of that relationship. Given the nature of the tradition as historical, the best place to begin our analysis proper is with a brief look back at the development of efforts to restrain particular weapons of war—for this forms the backdrop against which contemporary efforts must be viewed.

The "yes" given in just war tradition to the possibility of using violent means in the service of political ends has never been an absolute one, but has from its beginning been hedged about by the criteria of the traditional *jus ad bellum* and *jus in bello*.[5] Of the limits imposed, restraints on particular weapons or types of weapons have only rarely appeared. Possibly the most notable historical example was the canonical attempt, in the late eleventh and early twelfth centuries, to prohibit Christians from fighting one another with bows and arrows, crossbows, and siege weapons; there was no restriction, however, in the use of the weapons against non-Christians.[6] From later in the tradition one should surely mention Vattel's opinion that bombardment of cities with red-hot cannon balls, which had an indiscriminate incendiary effect, was a violation of noncombatant immunity,[7] and Locke's inveighing against means of war that have effects enduring after the war has ended, such as a scorched-earth policy might produce.[8] Consciously or unconsciously he echoed the biblical injunction (Deut. 20 : 19–20) against cutting down fruit trees and vineyards. Long a part of Western moral tradition on war, and read explicitly into the agenda of developing international law by Grotius,[9] was of course a more general type of prohibition regarding the use of poison in war, in particular that noncombatancy not be violated by the indiscriminate poisoning of water supplies and foodstuffs; the discriminating use of poison, as in an assassination, was another matter. (The Borgias, for all their evil qualities, did not violate Western custom when they poisoned their individual enemies.)

Notwithstanding these examples, efforts to restrict the actual weapons of war have not been a common feature of just war tradition through most of its history; only within the last century have such efforts multiplied rapidly. In the late nineteenth century religious and other pacifistic pressures begun to build against heavy artillery, but these might better be understood as attempts to shift the economic goods of society rather literally from guns to butter.[10] More specifically one might cite certain examples from international law: the St. Petersburg Declaration (1868) against small explosive projectiles, the Hague Declarations (1899) against expanding bullets and asphyxiating gases, the Washington Treaty (1922) relating to the use of submarines and noxious gases, the Protocol (1925) expanding the ban on gas warfare to include "asphyxiating, poisonous or other gases, and . . . bacteriological means of warfare," and the attempts over the last two decades to restrict use of chemical, bacteriological, and nuclear-thermonuclear weapons.[11] The antiballistic missile (ABM) and strategic arms limitation (SALT) treaties belong to this last group. There is certainly a moral component in these international conventions; yet the military and political components loom at least equally large.

One common factor in all these attempts at weapons restrictions has been the advancing technology of warfare, and the increased incidence of efforts in the last century to ban particular weapons can be correlated with the impact on warfare of the industrial, and later the scientific, revolution. With each new technological innovation has come a move to ban it from warfare. But it would be wrong to think that these moves have always or necessarily been moral in motivation or in effect. For example, a spirited and bitter resistance to firearms arose when these were introduced to the battlefield in the fifteenth and early sixteenth centuries. But this was not a moral outcry; it was the death rattle of chivalry, as the knightly class of Europe realized their vulnerability—both in formal war and outside it—to commoners armed with the harquebus.[12] A similar theme is recognizable in the nonproliferation treaty (NPT) of our own time, under which the existing nuclear powers have united with the aim of preserving their monopoly. The medieval ban on bows and siege weapons likewise appears to have been aimed, for the most part, not against these weapons as such but against professional soldiers—mercenaries—organized in specialized groups around the possession of such weapons and available at a price to all comers. Banning their weapons in intra-European warfare would, it was hoped, put an economic squeeze on the mercenaries and force them out of business—or at least into the wars against Islam, where their talents might be put to excellent use. The knightly class supported this move, along with peace-seeking ecclesiastics, because a mutual renunciation of the use of mercenaries among the knights amounted to a way to save money in their frequent armed hostilities with one another.[13] Again, I suggest, we might hear echoes of this attitude in contemporary debate over weapons restrictions.

But the point is that we need to assess correctly the moral implications of weapons control efforts, so that we might be in a better position to support or oppose particular efforts of this kind. I am convinced, moreover, that without such moral assessment society is in a poor position to make any intelligent judgment at all about the banning, permission, or restriction in use of particular types of weapons.

Consider, for example, how the general debate over technological progress has appeared historically in the context of innovations in weaponry. No less a figure than Francis Lieber, whom history remembers for his humanitarianism, looked with a quasi-scientific interest and with favor on new weapons introduced in the Civil War, such as the exploding bullet, because he reasoned that they would shorten the duration of the conflict.[14] That an opposite judgment on such bullets was written into international law a few years later, also in the name of humanitarianism, illustrates the difficulty here.[15] Arguments similar to Lieber's have been made before and since his time, and likewise similar arguments have been made to the contrary. Atomic bombs were used against Japan and defoliants in Vietnam partly for the reason cited be Lieber; similarly, even recognized limits of war have often been ignored because of this same reasoning. We Americans appear especially susceptible to it, whether out of our faith in technological and scientific progress or out of our system of government, which makes a lengthy, limited war hard to sustain politically; it is this that Ralph Potter, Robert W. Tucker, Russell Weigley, and others have identified as the "all or nothing" attitude, the "American way of war."[16] But, as our own time has abundantly revealed with regard to medicine, energy, and the environment, for every argument for the humanitarian benefits of scientific or technological progress there is a counterargument about its disutilities and even dangers; it is difficult—perhaps impossible—to settle the question of weapons restrictions on this ground. Yet this ground is precisely where much of the battle—historically and in the present day—has been fought. A perverse linkage exists between the reasoning of those who favor the "all"—no weapons limits, high defense budgets, the structure of military organization and strategic planning that anticipates unlimited efforts, should war come—and that of those who favor the "nothing"—a ban on nuclear arms, general disarmament, renunciation of war.[17]

By contrast, what wisdom having to do with restraints on weapons can be discerned in the traditional concepts associated with the just war idea? The overall thrust of this tradition is, of course, not so much to abolish war as to define limits or controls according to which war, as a recurrent phenomenon in historical life, can be made to serve certain moral purposes of a high and general nature. Such purposes include more just and peaceful relations among nations, an end to tyranny, and the protection and enhancement of innocent life. It would be foolish to claim that these ends have been achieved, in any full, unambiguous sense, in any war in human history; yet it is equally absurd to deny the effect of the tradition, defined as a consensual set of purposes and outer restraints on warfare, in limiting the harm done by such organized, state-sponsored violence.

In terms of the theoretical structure of the tradition, restraints on particular types of weapons belong to the *jus in bello;* there they overlap both the principles, discrimination and proportionality, that define the moral notion of *jus in bello.*[18]

The problem of moral analysis of weapons restriction is complicated by limiting factors that have to do with strategic, tactical, or legal considerations. This leads to certain apparently irresolvable dilemmas.

For example, in terms of just war analysis the ideal strategic force might well be described as one that is designedly defensive. Leaving aside the question of justified offensive use of force, which is permitted under certain conditions, the tradition clearly puts a high priority on defensive measures of one sort or another—either truly defensive, on the model of warding off a blow already launched, or retaliatory. A totally efficient strategic defense, one that would ward off all attacks, would leave no need for retaliation. Such a defense would turn a nation into the corporate human equivalent of a turtle, or an armadillo, or perhaps at most a porcupine. By contrast, defense by strategic deterrence, whether by nuclear missiles or other means, would seem to be analogous in the animal world to the threat of retaliation posed by the tiger or the rattlesnake. In either case the message is, "Don't tread on me." But the retaliatory threat, when it is based on thermonuclear missiles targeted at a potential enemy's cities, is a threat to do something grotesquely immoral. It has, of course, been debated whether to threaten to do something immoral is itself an immoral act, especially when the threat is designed to deter the potential enemy from an immoral countercity nuclear strike, and allowing for the additional (though unlikely) consideration that we might never carry through on our own threatened retaliation. Such is the nuclear dilemma, and the results of the moral debate have never been wholly satisfactory.[19] But in any case, a truly defensive strategy, one based on blunting or warding off an enemy's offensive strike, would appear to be the morally superior goal. And this poses another kind of nuclear dilemma.

Truly defensive methods, as I am using this term, would include civil defense measures and some sort of weaponry designed to disable incoming missiles—ideally, to explode them in space, at the apex of their ballistic trajectory, before they reentered the atmosphere. But either defensive scheme, or some combination of the two, would have to be developed over a period of years, and that very development would be a destabilizing measure that would increase the risk of nuclear war by undermining the principle of mutual assured destruction on which current nuclear stability rests.[20] That is, the results of such a defensive scheme might be morally worthwhile, but getting there poses such risks as to be seriously questionable both morally and politically. This was what was wrong with the antiballistic missile effort of a decade ago—quite apart from the fact that the ABMs in question were far from being a truly effective defense system. Though at first look a defensive strategy based on the ABM idea appeared morally superior to that based on a retaliatory threat, on closer inspection its peculiar form of the nuclear dilemma emerged. The ABM Treaty of 1972, by severely limiting ABM deployment, insured the continuation of deterrent force stability; neither side could hope to create a situation in which it could outstrip the other in defensive means so that it could launch a preemptive strike in confidence that the retaliation would be ineffective. Thus in this instance an arms limitation treaty that from one perspective appears morally retrograde turns out, from another perspective, to have been a good thing.

But, in an attempt to understand the general problem of arms control more fully, let us shift focus away from nuclear weapons for a moment to consider the matter of incapacitating gases. These, along with other chemical and bacteriological means of war, are banned by international convention.[21] Understanding this case of prohibited weapons may help us, by analogy, better to comprehend the moral, political, and military dynamics of efforts to impose limits on nuclear weapons.

It is certainly conceivable that an incapacitating gas might, in certain instances, offer the most humane—that is, the least destructive—means of disabling an enemy. Where the alternative is to disable a soldier by shooting him, incinerating him with napalm, or irradiating him, an incapacitating gas with temporary effect, followed by the imprisonment of the enemy force, would seem to be more in line with the just war principle—as ancient as Augustine—of inflicting the least harm necessary to prevent the enemy from accomplishing his own goals. Paul Ramsey's discussion of this argument for the particular context of Vietnam[22] is well known, and I will not attempt to develop it further here. But I do wish to point up some features of this sort of case that are generally poorly understood. First, it is beside the point that in actual use in Vietnam the use of asphyxiating gases was regularly followed by the shooting of those affected and not their imprisonment. It has long been a principle of international law that wounded soldiers who make no resistance are not to be further harmed but rather made prisoners of war. We could learn to employ asphyxiating gases in this way. Instead, what is generally wrong with the use of chemical and bacteriological means of war from a moral standpoint—and this is my second point—is the difficulty of limiting their effects to combatants. This is why, as I read just war tradition, the poisoning of wells has been so regularly and repeatedly condemned. It is not the nature of the means that has been prohibited, but the use. Similarly with contemporary chemical and bacteriological means of war: if such means could be developed so that their effects could be controlled at least as much, say, as gunfire, the analogy with poisoning a well would disappear. It is just this, I think, that has kept napalm off the list of prohibited chemical weapons of war, in spite of its horrendous effect on those persons who become its direct or indirect target. By contrast a temporarily asphyxiating gas is much more humane in its short-term and long-term effects; yet it resembles too much the case of a poisoned well, since it tends to drift about and indiscriminately affect everyone in the area of its employment.

Yet there remains a third point to consider about chemical and bacteriological weapons, a point that does not appear to have directly to do with morality at all but which has been at the core of arms control efforts over history. This is the practical problem of an effective defense, coupled with the fact of mutual possession of such weapons. Both the Washington Treaty of 1922 and the 1925 Protocol banning gas warfare were framed in conscious reaction to the experience of World War I, in which both sides had made use of chlorine and mustard gas. As used in that war, the problem with the gas weapon was not discrimination; noncombatants were well away from the stable, trench-defined front lines where the gases were released. Nor does it appear to have been the lasting effects of the particular gases used, since a veteran with lungs scarred by mustard gas might seem relatively whole by comparison with one who had lost one or more limbs to shellfire or machine gun bullets. Rather the controlling factor appears to have been that the only really effective defense against the gas weapon was the threat of retaliation in kind. A humanitarian reaction against the effect of gas certainly formed a part of the background of the Washington Treaty; yet in the foreground was the willingness of the signatory nations to give up a weapon that not only was hard to control in actual use but was highly destructive, relatively easy and cheap to possess, and extremely hard to defend against. In other words, the real guarantor of the effectiveness of the treaty and its appended protocol was the threat of retaliation in kind; that continues to be, in my mind, the guarantor today.

Thus there turns out in the ban on gas warfare to be the same sort of dilemma as is present with nuclear weaponry: what is objectionable in terms of moral principle becomes tolerable from the perspective of a calculus of efficacy weighed against the likelihood of retaliation. But the resolution in the two cases has been somewhat different: the treaty ban on gases has been strengthened by subsequent prohibitions directed against chemical and bacteriological weapons generally, with but a few exceptions,[23] while nuclear arms agreements have permitted growth of strategic stockpiles and development of new tactical weapons as well.[24] In the simplest terms, even with mutual possession and no real defense against either chemical and bacteriological weapons or nuclear weapons, the resolution in the former case has been at a relatively low level of political and monetary cost and public danger, while that in the latter has permitted— even fostered—higher and higher costs, in terms both of money spent and goods and services forgone, and apparently greater and greater public danger, as we are reminded by reflecting on how many times the world can be destroyed by present levels of strategic weaponry.

This is an ironic and puzzling difference, and I admit I have no ready explanation for it. Indeed, from the standpoint of logic, there seems no reason why the two cases should not have been resolved similarly. But before we side with logic over history, we should realize that there is no good logical reason why a similar resolution should have been on the model of the treatment of gas warfare; we might equally well expect the opposite kind of resolution, so that there would not exist great arsenals of chemical and bacteriological agents, amassed and maintained at great cost and having the potential of destroying the world's life many times over. If history has been inconsistent, it is at least batting .667 where nuclear, chemical, and bacteriological weapons are concerned.

Still, we could hope for an effective treaty ban on nuclear weapons as well, and we need further to consider the dissimilar histories of these dissimilar cases. I have mentioned three characteristics of incapacitating gases as a weapon that made them likely targets for an arms control agreement: their indiscriminacy and difficulty of control in actual use, their relative ease and cheapness of production, so that any power, no matter how immature or irresponsible its leadership, could create its own gas doomsday weapon, and the near impossibility of an effective defense. I further have argued that these three characteristics now apply to nuclear weapons as well. To elaborate this point a bit, not only their immediate blast and radiation effect but the lingering radioactivity they leave behind make them indiscriminate, while no one really knows whether sophisticated electronic guidance systems will work under combat conditions or be thrown off by the radio-wave activity of previous nuclear explosions;[25] the plans for making a nuclear device have become generally available, and the materials may be had by various means, legitimate and illegitimate; and no truly effective defense against such weapons exists. But these three characteristics were not always in effect, and herein lies the difference in how nuclear weapons have been treated as compared with chemical and bacteriological ones—the paradigm case being that of asphyxiating gases. In the first place, as Michael Mandelbaum has recently argued, the early atomic bombs were not conceived as radical departures from the high explosives already in use in World War II; it was not until the invention of the hydrogen bomb that a realization began to dawn that nuclear weaponry was of a quite different sort from what had gone before.[26] In the second place, the relative ease with which a nuclear device can be constructed today is a very recent development, a matter of the last few years. Initially the United States was the only power to possess nuclear weapons, and even now there are only five recognized nuclear powers, though there certainly exists a handful more. So the first two of the three characteristics I have identified were not there in the beginning in the case of nuclear weapons; what about the third, defense? The answer is the same: only with the introduction of the ballistic missile as the primary delivery system for nuclear warheads has the possibility of an effective defense disappeared. Hardened missile sites, nuclear submarines, mobile land-based missles, and cruise missiles all increase the difficulty of defense and make actual use of strategic nuclear weapons undesirable. Thus none of the three characteristics that made asphyxiating gases—and by extension other chemical and bacteriological agents—so susceptible to banning were present for nuclear weapons in the beginning; these characteristics have only gradually emerged for such weapons, and the factors that have produced them continue to develop.

Several not entirely happy results follow from this sort of comparative analysis—unhappy both because they fly in the face of much of the feeling that motivates contemporary popular efforts to effect arms control and limitation and because they appear to contradict the limiting moral principles of just war tradition as well. For one thing, this analysis suggests that increasing the possibility of nuclear proliferation—which is quite a different thing from increasing proliferation itself—may be a good thing. Not all powers in 1922 or 1925 possessed a gas warfare capability, but all could have obtained one relatively cheaply and straightforwardly. The situation is, I think, the same with nuclear weapons today and is likely to become even more so with the growth in availability of fissionable products in the future. In the second place, the comparison suggests that it was right to ban ABMs and, generally, to do whatever is possible to maintain the superiority of the offensive over the defensive in relation to nuclear weapons. As noted earlier, this sits poorly with the just war notion of what is right in war—the *jus in bello*. Third, this analysis also suggests that the arms race itself, while costly and dangerous in the short run, may not be a bad thing to have happened in the long run. This is clearly at odds with the sentiments expressed by nongovernmental organizations and private individuals who understand arms control to mean at least an end to the arms race and wish to see positive arms reduction beyond that. Let us look at these implications more closely.

As to the first point, that nuclear proliferation may be in some way actually desirable from the standpoint of arms control efforts, I think what leads to this position is the idea that undesirable weapons must reach a kind of "critical mass" in the armament systems of the nations of the world before any meaningful, consensual effort to limit or ban their use can be carried through to success. As I have indicated, actual possession by a large plurality of powers is not the principal issue, but rather the ability to possess the weapon in question relatively easily and cheaply. Gas clearly fitted this description, and ease of possession was enhanced by the ready convertibility of chemical plants from producing industrial or agricultural chemicals to weapons. Indeed, for chlorine, one widely used gas in World War I, no conversion was necessary, as chlorine is itself used in a wide variety of civilian applications. With nuclear weapons there is a similar linkage, this time with nuclear power plants and especially with breeder reactors, which as a consequence of their design produce quantities of weapons-grade fissionable materials along with lower-grade fuel for nuclear power plants. The hunger of third world nations for nuclear power can, with unhappy ease, be transformed into the quest for nuclear weapons capability—as has already apparently happened in India, Israel, and South Africa and seems on the verge of happening in Pakistan, with Libyan support. Again, the comparison I have made between gas and nuclear weapons appears to suggest that allowing nuclear proliferation to continue may be, in the long run, the best course toward achieving controls on such weapons, and the desires of third world nations appear to underscore this argument.

But nonetheless, this argument is seriously flawed. In the first place, the analogy is by no means so close as I have made it. In 1922 and 1925 the shape of international law was still defined by a relatively few powerful, industrialized nations, who were able to effect arms control agreements in rather the same way as they could control trade. The world today is far more fragmented, and world politics are confused by the fact of differences among third world nations that are at least as great as those between them, as a group, and the major powers. *Proliferation* in 1922 and 1925, as applied to chemical and bacteriological weapons, meant possession or potential possession by a handful of powers with governments and traditions of government at least apparently stable enough to ensure compliance. Today, even aside from the obvious problem of an atomic bomb in the hands of a Qaddafi, there is the matter of international terrorism and the justifiable fear that nuclear proliferation will result in the use or threat of use of a nuclear weapon by a terrorist group for its own ends. In terms of great-power possession of nuclear weapons, the world is already well beyond where it was in 1922 or 1925 with regard to gas warfare capabilities, and so if the analogy suggests anything, it should be to point away from further nuclear proliferation toward genuine control and limitation of these weapons.

There is a further matter bearing on the flaw in the argument that proliferation to a critical mass is necessary before control efforts can succeed; this is the fact that what such a critical mass is rests on judgment, not on some immutable scientific (or social-scientific) law. Here the function of just war tradition as a source of moral values to inform judgment comes into its own, and the use of that tradition to inform and educate moral opinion is indicated. What is wrong with nuclear weapons should not be put solely in terms of their sheer power to destroy human life but also in terms of their inherent indiscriminacy, and much more serious attention must be given to alternative weapons and weapons systems that, if developed, would afford more moral ways for nations to protect the interests of their citizens and of the world community itself. Arms control efforts which fail to recognize this latter need for genuinely effective weaponry adapted to legitimate uses simply represent a break with the moral wisdom of the past, as preserved in just war tradition. The requirement in this country that the Judge Advocate General's office approve each new military weapon after proposal but before development and again after development but before deployment represents, from the standpoint of just war thought, a genuinely moral step—considerably more moral than a utopian "ban the bomb" effort that takes no thought of the consequences of its proposals for increasing the chance of nuclear war by undermining deterrent stability.

To return to the original analogy between gas and nuclear weapons, another implication I earlier drew from that analogy was that, in the long run, the arms race may not turn out to have been entirely a bad thing to have happened. I was not, of course, speaking of the long run as defined by John Maynard Keynes, in which "we are all dead." Rather I meant to suggest that the nuclear arms race has functioned and is, in the view of most strategic analysts, increasingly functioning as a way of imposing an effective limit on the actual use of the nuclear weapons stockpiled. One of the most straightforward recent explorations of this concept has been advanced by Michael Mandelbaum under the rubric of a "nuclear regime for the future."[27] Mandelbaum argues the case that the greatest deterrent to nuclear war is the assured ability to retaliate. This is a familiar case, but what is new in his argument is the effort he expends on showing how alternative "regimes for the future" are, because based on a less sure or less stable deterrent, more dangerous for the world.

Following this line of argument, we see that what is most important is the *balance* of forces rather than any specific level of total force available. Given the inherent dangers of nuclear weapons, though, there exist incentives to establish lower and lower levels of balance; at the same time, these dangers plus the monetary costs of escalation combine to testify to the advantages of avoiding escalation to new and higher levels of total force, assuming the preservation of balance. Merely keeping a balance was the goal of both the SALT and MLBF (multi-lateral balanced force) negotiations, and indeed any nuclear arms limitation negotiations in the contemporary context must assume this aim. But this is no longer enough. The critical mass, in the sense I have been using it, has long since been achieved, and now the problem is how to move to genuine arms limitation without destroying the balance of forces necessary to prevent war. A familiar technique in physics is to suspend a particle between two electromagnetic fields; providing that the fields are powerful enough to suspend the particle at all, they must then be kept carefully balanced at whatever level of power is chosen in order to keep the particle from falling out of suspension. Delicate as this problem is in physics, it is far more delicate in international relations, and the stakes are far higher.

We are now living in the "long run" mentioned above, when competition in nuclear weapons has become centered on ensuring the invulnerability of the strategic retaliatory force. This, rather than raw numbers of weapons, is the model for maintaining the necessary balance of forces in the future. On this analysis, the arms race turned a corner some time ago and, so far as nuclear weapons are concerned, is now directed to ensure their nonuse. The increasing disutility of these weapons, reflected in the treaty agreements, has already effected a de facto ban, and whether a de jure ban ever comes into being or not, it is this disutility that stands as the strongest barrier against nuclear war.

Still there remains that nagging problem of the incompatibility between the just war *jus in bello* and dependence on a strategic deterrent aimed at noncombatants. Posed in terms of this incompatibility, this is a dilemma of classic proportions. Resolution toward either of these incompatible alternatives means giving up the benefits of the other. But perhaps, as some theorists argue, it is inappropriate to think of a deterrent force in the same way that we must think of one designed to be used; that is, suppose there really is a difference between tactical weaponry and the strategic nuclear arsenal. Strategic analysts have been saying this for years, but ethical analysis, blinded by fascination with an insoluble dilemma or ready to resolve that dilemma against the nuclear arsenal whatever the consequences, has not taken the implications of the strategic–tactical difference sufficiently seriously. But doing so offers a way out of the dilemma that preserves and, ideally, strengthens both its horns. Let us consider the descriptions that have regularly been advanced of the strategic nuclear force: again and again recur the assurances that it is built *not* to be used, that if the occasion should ever arise for its use, the war will have already been lost, so that it would be irrational to use it. What the strategic arsenals of enormous potential destructiveness are, according to such descriptions, is the contemporary equivalent of a medieval castle wall. The difference— and it is real—is that the contemporary deterrent is designed *only* to deter attack, while the fortress wall was designed not only to deter potential enemies but also to defend securely against an actual attack. Deterrence is now, as it was in the fourteenth century and has always been, a mental barrier. Though resting on physical realities—the thickness of a castle wall, the size of an enemy's army and its readiness for war, the ability of an enemy's economy to stand up to war—it has in the end never been more than a mental barrier kept in place by a counting of the costs by putative belligerents. An efficacious deterrent is at least as good, in moral terms, as an efficacious defense, and better too. While defense can only prevent the evil in progress from reaching its conclusion, and while retaliation can only retake something lost and punish the taker, an efficacious deterrent means preventing the evil in the first place.

Now, this perspective on strategic nuclear weapons still does not remove the grave moral problem with their actual use in a war. That remains; it comes from the inherent indiscriminacy and disproportionality of such weapons when targeted on population centers. Nor does it counter the realistic fear that, if reliance on deterrent forces becomes too heavy, in event of war these morally unusable weapons will in fact be employed. From the standpoint of the just war tradition's *jus in bello* the dilemma of strategic nuclear weapons— which is the dilemma of their use, or threat of use, in counterpopulation warfare—remains in all its force. But from the *jus ad bellum* perspective it is possible to see that moral and practical considerations point the same way—toward an effective deterrent to war. And thus far nuclear strategic deterrence has been remarkably effective—ironically, a much better barrier to war than the Kellogg-Briand Treaty of 1927, the "agreement to abolish war," whose effect endured with manifest fragility for only a decade.

In these comments I am not attempting to put a rosy face

on the grim visage of death nor trying to explain away the moral objections to nuclear weapons in particular or war in general. Rather I am trying to suggest that so long as war remains possible—that is, so long as the eschaton is not yet here—moral purposes may sometimes best be achieved by not entirely savory means. In this regard the continued existence and enhancement of nuclear deterrent forces, including the progressive development of less massively destructive means of deterrence and alongside the provision of effective means of defense and war-fighting capability, is the lesser evil not only politically and militarily, but also morally. Recent and pending arms control agreements should be judged similarly, as representing the lesser of evils and thus as a positive good relative to the requirements of history.

III
Strategic and Tactical Planning

5

Weapons, Tactics, and Morality in War

In a suggestive recent analysis on which I have already drawn, Michael Mandelbaum has described the development of modern war in terms of three revolutions: the Napoleonic, the industrial, and the atomic.[1] The first of these, as depicted by Mandelbaum, transformed the face of war by making the goals not the petty personal ends of individual sovereigns, who fought war as a kind of game, but the goals of an entire people fired by an ideologically defined vision; by hugely increasing the size of armies through conscription; and by restructuring the national economy so as to function in support of the military in time of war. The second made available weapons of much greater destructive power in far larger quantities than thought possible in earlier ages; the third prolongs the first two but, through producing deterrence strategy, holds the promise of eliminating war, else it may bring a nuclear holocaust. While useful and in many ways persuasive, this conception of the development of modern war smacks of historical inevitability, as war moves increasingly away from the prospect of restraint to the point where no *in bello* limits are thought possible.

Similarly, in his *The Great War and Modern Memory*, Paul Fussell describes the memory of World War I in terms of the symbolic expectation that all war must be as that one was perceived by the men in the front-line trenches: chaotic, uncontrolled, without reasonable purpose, horribly and totalistically destructive. This interpretation too carries the taste of inevitability: by thinking of war in terms of the experience of the last one, we are doomed to make of memory a self-fulfilling prophecy about what war must be.[2]

Other contemporary critics make similar judgments.[3] Yet while these judgments have a certain ring of truth to them, it is only retrospectively and from a restricted perspective on history that they can withstand critical testing. Not all wars since Napoleon have been fought by national armies of conscripts, supported by the nation at large, for goals of an ideological nature. Not all wars since the industrial revolution began have employed the latest and most destructive technology available, nor applied to combat the entirety of means in national military arsenals. And there is nothing inevitable in the development of nuclear weaponry that necessitates a strategic standoff complemented by the prospect of a general holocaust. Similarly, the expectation of totalistic, uncontrolled warfare has not been borne out in practice: not only is it doubtful—contrary to Fussell—that World War I should be thought of entirely this way, but the experience of limited war since 1945 flows directly counter to the idea that symbolic expectation in the twentieth century requires all-out wars.[4]

The flow of history is not predetermined, nor is it inevitable that historical developments will continue along lines already laid down—especially if account is taken of the tensions that in fact shape the movement of history at every stage. Thus even if we grant—as I think we must, in honesty—that the overall conception of the purposes of war, of its weapons and its tactics has in the modern period undermined the practical possibility of fighting discriminately and proportionately, it is nonetheless possible to change this state of affairs in the future. The restraint of war has prospered in some ages of the past, while losing ground in others; yet in every age the picture is mixed, with a persistent tension between tendencies toward all-out warfare and warfare held in check by humanly imposed restraints. This is no less true in our own age: besides the development of limited war theory and practice, the last century has produced the most extensive international legal efforts to control war and its impact that history has witnessed since the time, three to four centuries ago, of Victoria, Suarez, Gentili, and Grotius.[5] Thus the picture before us at this point in history is not unrelievedly black, as the most pessimistic critics of war argue; indeed, to the contrary, this may be the time when it is possible to ask most seriously how to make operational for contemporary warfare the ideas of restraint traditionally expressed as proportionality and discrimination.[6]

The totalistic practice of war is dictated by the assumption that the purposes of war must be total and unconditional. This assumption has certainly been much in evidence in the warfare of the twentieth century, notably in the two world wars and in the East–West Cold War. But there is nothing inevitable or a priori about this view of war. If we start instead from the assumption that some circumstances may come into being in which the use of force is necessary to protect or preserve certain values—the fundamental rationale of just war tradition, and a position on which such diverse thinkers as Augustine and Clausewitz agree—then we are required to think about how to structure military doctrine and the weapons of war to fit.

It is useful to begin by thinking some hard thoughts about the wrong way to proceed—hard because of the seductiveness of the way of thinking we must reject. This is the idea that the best war is the shortest one, and everything that can be done to shorten armed conflict ought to be done. Like most clichés of thought, this idea has some truth to it. A protracted conflict may spread to involve an ever wider circle of belligerents. Further, a drawn-out conflict may escalate, as each belligerent suffers more and tries to make the other pay for the harm it has inflicted. Similarly, the people of a belligerent nation may come to feel that the price they have paid over a long conflict justifies winning at all costs. Thus a long war may become a wider war in which greater and greater pressures arise for unlimited prosecution and fighting to the death.

If this were all that could be said, then the claim that the shortest war is the best would have to stand, and the means of war that produced the briefest conflicts would have to be judged the most moral. But this is not all there is to say. First, a long war may produce the adverse developments mentioned, or it may not; history provides examples on both sides, and there is nothing inevitable about either a short war being relatively more sweet or a long one relatively more bitter. Second, all the factors mentioned are, at least in principle, under human control: it is possible by careful management of a conflict and sustained diplomatic effort to keep it from spreading; further, such management, along with the avoidance of inflammatory rhetoric and the creation of expectations about victory that are both too high and false, works to reduce pressure toward adopting totalistic means and a fight-to-the-death attitude. Third, the argument that the shortest war is always the best rests ultimately on a calculation of proportionality, and the claim is thus that the shortest war is best because it produces the least harm. This is extremely hard to sustain, however. In the present context a brief strategic missile exchange between the United States and the Soviet Union would certainly be the shortest war in history; yet it would be more destructive than the most protracted conventional wars the world has known, and even a limited nuclear war could be waged for a lengthy period without producing the destruction that such a spasmodic thermonuclear exchange would create.

But perhaps the greatest difficulty with the position that war must be made as short as possible by whatever means available is that this approach, far more than the drawing out of conflict over a longer period, makes for escalation in the immoral destructiveness of war. Some examples will illustrate this. First, recall the case of Francis Lieber, who during the American Civil War, even as he was engaged in drafting the first United States Army manual on the law of war, singled out with approval the introduction of exploding bullets by the Union Army, reasoning that they would shorten the war by incapacitating more soldiers.[7] There is no evidence that they shortened the war, but these projectiles did increase the suffering of everyone they hit by showering small fragments of metal all over the body. Similarly Maxim, the inventor of the first reliable machine gun, believed it was a humanitarian weapon that would, because of its destructiveness, cause wars to be much shorter and might even lead to the disappearance of war from history. World War I gave the lie to this expectation; ironically, it was the machine gun that kept another effort at a quick victory, the charge across no-man's-land, from succeeding. Again and again these two latter representatives of the "briefer is always better" approach to war nullified each other, meanwhile creating human carnage unlike anything before in military history. The great fallacy of World War II centered on aerial strategic bombing, which was held by its proponents to promise a shorter war by undermining civilian support for the enemy's warmaking efforts.[8] What such bombing certainly did was vastly raise the level of harm to noncombatants; it is not at all clear that similar bombing directed against military targets would not have been a more effective way to reduce the enemy's military potential. The atomic bombing of Hiroshima and Nagasaki was but an extension of this counterpopulation aerial bombing strategy, no different in principle from the air attacks on London, Hamburg, Dresden, and Tokyo; only the weapon was different—another weapon that, like the dream Maxim had for the machine gun, promised to bring a quick end to war. But what aerial counterpopulation bombing in fact achieved was to violate not only the moral principle of discrimination but also that of proportion, for such means of war made sense only when all enemies were regarded (wrongly) as combatants and the ends of war were defined (wrongly) as great enough to justify all possible means.

Finally, lest the villain in this discussion be identified too closely with the introduction of new, "decisive" weapons of war, let me stress again that the use of available weapons must also be taken into account. What is wrong and must be avoided is the seductive but fundamentally incorrect and immoral view that shorter conflicts, even if sharper, are always to be sought over longer ones, and that any and all

means that promise to shorten a conflict are therefore justified. What is wrong here is not the desire to shorten armed
conflicts when they do break out; it is the assumption that
such shortening is the chief goal to be served, along with the
corollary reasoning that justifies totalistic means in the service of this end.

There is, on the other hand, no reason either to favor
protracted conflicts as such over shorter ones. The issue is to
hold the use of military force within moral limits and thus
to make sure that the political ideals which such force serves
are themselves framed in morally justifiable terms, while
also providing weapons of war and training in the means of
war that are in principle capable of being kept under the
control of moral intentionality. The wars of the twentieth
century have provided enough examples of error in all these
areas, and the errors found there suggest their own solution:
avoidance of ultimate goals and ultimate means of war in
favor of goals and means defined by the ideas of limitation,
relativity, and control.

Two recent weapons added to the American arsenal represent a turn in this direction: the cruise missile and the
"neutron," or enhanced radiation, warhead. While the latter
has already been discussed briefly in a previous chapter,
these two weapons deserve a closer look, both in terms of
their own inherent capabilities and in terms of the possible
uses that might be made of them in actual military conflict.
In the immediate context the purpose of this examination is
to assess the potential for restrained, controlled use of these
weapons as compared to those they replace; yet farther into
the future, what we can learn from this brief inquiry may
offer suggestions as to how to continue to change the shape
of warfare in the direction of increased discrimination and
proportionality in the means of war.

The Neutron Warhead

While conventional weapons rely on blast and heat effect for
their destructive power, nuclear weapons add the effects of
radiation to blast and heat damage. When the first atomic

bombs were developed, it was still blast and heat effect that was sought; the advantage of atomic weapons was understood to be that they could create a far more powerful explosion, measured in these conventional terms, than was possible by the same weight or volume of conventional high explosive. Radiation was a collateral effect, but it did not represent the reason for developing atomic weaponry, and exploitation of the radiation produced in nuclear fission was not attempted in the early development of these weapons. This approach to atomic weaponry was symbolically expressed in the decision to rate their power in terms of kilotons or, later, megatons of TNT. It was also expressed in the uses for which atomic weapons were developed, which represented simply a prolongation of ideas for the use of conventional high-explosive bombs. Nor did matters change when fusion weapons came onto the scene: in these the ratio of blast and heat effect to the size of the warhead was far greater than in fission weapons, and it was this pronounced improvement in blast and heat on which military thinking seized. What was superior about fusion weapons over fission warheads was precisely what made fission weapons superior to conventional high explosives: a vast increase in the kind of damage conventional weapons produced—damage from blast and heat. Though radiation also increased by a striking amount in fusion explosions, strategically and tactically the radiation effects of both fission and fusion weapons remained a side effect not much taken into account in planning. Indeed, perhaps the kindest face that can be put on United States military tests some thirty years ago that deliberately exposed unprotected soldiers to radiation from nuclear blasts is that it simply was not expected that this radiation would make an appreciable difference, not only in the military efficiency of the troops immediately after the detonation, but in their lives over the long run. This military attitude was mirrored in the civilian society, where too, well into the second decade of the atomic age, the possibility of radiation damage was considered far less important than the potential atomic power held for the improvement of life. The present depth of concern over atomic radiation, sometimes approaching paranoia, is simply the reverse side of this earlier studied avoidance of radiation effect.

Tactical fission and strategic fusion weapons of current types represent developments that are analogous to conventional high explosive; that is, they were designed chiefly for the blast effect they could produce, thereby substituting for conventional blast weapons. Radiation was ignored. Now, though, it is no longer possible to ignore the detrimental radiation effects that would follow from the use of such weapons. Still, if it were possible to modify these weapons so that the same blast and heat effect remained but the radiation disappeared, this would not alter their functions at all.

The neutron warhead, by contrast, represents an attempt to exploit radiation effect as compared with blast and heat, and thus it marks a genuine departure from thinking incubated in the days when high explosive was king in warfare—notably the two world wars. Not a pure radiation weapon by any means, this is rather a miniaturized fusion warhead with effects characteristic of the larger strategic warheads, though proportionately smaller. This implies by comparison with tactical fission weapons far greater emission of harmful radiation for a given yield (that is, level of blast and heat effect, measured in terms of kilo- or megatonnage of conventional TNT). Neutron radiation is especially enhanced; hence the nickname "neutron bomb." But neutron radiation is not long-enduring, so that the lingering effect of radioactive contamination in the area of the explosion is diminished—again, by comparison with the dominant types of radiation caused by a fission blast of similar yield.

Now, is there anything of moral significance in all this? The answer is yes, maybe, depending on how the neutron weapon is used. The response we make is also conditioned by whether we give priority to the idea of discrimination or to proportionality in judging the effects of this weapon.

The neutron warhead has been publicly described as fundamentally an antiarmor weapon, designed to kill or incapacitate the crews of armored vehicles by means of the radiation that would penetrate their armored defenses. More broadly, the purpose of this weapon may be understood through its effect of killing or incapacitating all persons (indeed, all organic life) in the target area within a short time after detonation, while causing property damage limited by comparison to the effect of tactical fusion or large conventional warheads used to the same end in the same target area. All persons in the target area who are not protected against neutron radiation will suffer its effects; this weapon is indiscriminate over its area of effectiveness. In practice, people not killed outright would be incapacitated by radiation sickness within minutes or hours, with death following within a day for most persons affected.

If we begin to assess these effects from the standpoint of the primacy of discrimination, understood as an absolute prohibition of direct, intentional harm to noncombatants, we must first insist that the means of war allow distinguishing between these persons and combatants. Some weapons are inherently more capable of being used discriminatingly than others; at the lower end of the scale of destructiveness, for example, a rifle is a more discriminate weapon than a shotgun or a machine gun. Where antitank weapons are at issue, a wire-guided missile is clearly superior in these moral terms to any larger weapon whose effects blanket a far greater area. Yet the particular use to which a rifle or a wire-guided missile is put may be indiscriminate: random sniping in a crowded shopping area, for example, or using such a missile against a school bus loaded with children. The concept of discrimination remains in the first instance a moral term defining the choice made in a particular instance to use a given weapon or not, or to use it in one way as opposed to another. Yet the adaptability of a weapon to discriminating use is also morally relevant, for some weapons are virtually impossible to use with discrimination in most imaginable circumstances. In this regard the enhanced radiation warhead may have an advantage not possessed by the tactical fission and high-explosive warheads it presumably would displace. But to explore this possibility we must leave behind the idea that direct, intentional effect also means *immediate* effect; we must consider the long-term effects on noncombatants that can be foreseen and calculated and that can therefore be weighed in the scales of directness and intentionality.

What distinguishes the neutron warhead, in this context, from the other types it would replace is the relatively smaller long-term effect it is described as having. Specifically, less property damage and less long-term residual radiation are expected. Let us consider the ideal type of situation in which this weapon might be used in a limited nuclear war: the target is a certain military force, made up and disposed in such a way that a neutron warhead would be the most militarily effective means of force available, located in an area from which all noncombatants have previously fled. Here the possibility of direct, intentional harm to noncombatants is lacking, and the principle of discrimination is therefore satisfied, in terms of immediate effect. But let us assume further that the blast damage that would be caused by conventional high explosive or tactical fission warheads sufficient to accomplish the military mission, along with the residual radiation left behind by the latter weapons, would substantially outweigh the blast and residual radiation damage caused by the neutron weapon. These sorts of long-term harm to property and to an environment on which people depend for the conditions of normal living are morally significant from the standpoint of observing noncombatant immunity. After the wave of war has passed and the noncombatant inhabitants of this target area return to their homes and work, the property destruction and the radiation danger they will encounter will undoubtedly affect them in their attempts once more to pick up their lives, and so these forms of damage are significant factors in determining whether any nondiscriminating harm to noncombatants has occurred. From the perspective of discrimination the long-term effects of particular weapons are thus relevant, as the amount and types of such effects help to determine whether the intention was in fact to disregard the rights of noncombatants, either immediately or through the lasting impact of the weapon on their lives, or whether the damage caused to noncombatants was, by the moral rule of double effect, a secondary and indirect result of a permitted action against combatants. In cases like the one sketched here the possibility does seem to exist that in some conditions the neutron weapon can be used with greater moral discrimination than tactical fission weapons and even conventional high explosives.

Shifting perspective to the question of proportionality, we can employ the same considerations to argue that the total level of damage is likely to be less with the neutron weapon than with the other two types it would displace. The effect on military personnel is, of course, expected to be as great with the new weapon as with the other types; its advantage over conventional high explosives and tactical fission weapons is its lowered damage to property, while compared to the latter it also promises less long-term danger to life from radiation left after the blast. If account is taken of the total effect on the belligerent populations, in particular on those people whose homes and livelihoods are found in combat areas, the new weapon emerges as possibly a more proportionate means of waging modern war.

Still, though, there remains the question of whether other weapons now available might be both more discriminating and more proportionate. The answer is yes, and if we assume equivalent military efficacy, these other weapons should accordingly be the ones employed. Put most radically, to *kill* even enemy soldiers is not the end of war; that end is to protect or preserve values that cannot otherwise be served than by the use of force. If weapons could be devised that would only temporarily incapacitate and that could be used in the contexts typical of war directly and intentionally against combatants while avoiding harm to noncombatants, these would accordingly be ideal. Regarded from this perspective, a temporarily incapacitating chemical or biological weapon might well be the most proportionate, though difficult to use with discrimination. Without going so far, we may infer from reflecting on the need to use restraint in war that the most discriminating and proportionate weapons should be those of first resort, while the least discriminating and proportionate should be those last chosen. Strategy and tactics, along with training and military dispositions, should be framed accordingly. At the same time, as already argued in an earlier chapter, emphasis in weapons research and development should be placed on devising weapons of equal or greater effectiveness compared to those now deployed, but inherently more proportionate and discriminating. The qualified approval here given to the neutron weapon follows from its apparently being such a weapon as this—one better than those it replaces in a moral sense, though still raising significant moral problems. But steps in the right direction must be taken when they may, even if they are only short steps.

Before leaving the subject of the neutron weapon, we must examine the implications of the assumption made earlier that noncombatants will not be in the area of use of this weapon. What if noncombatants are present? Moreover, if use of this weapon (and others also available) depends on the removal of noncombatants, is the creation of a "free-fire" zone a moral option? Four considerations will help to clarify what is at stake here.

1. If avoidance of direct, intentional harm to noncombatants is taken seriously as one of the values to be served in warfare, then the presence of noncombatants in a battle area may inhibit the use of certain kinds of weapons, namely those that are most indiscriminate in their effects. Where bonds of commonalty exist across the lines of belligerency, the greatest likelihood exists of mutual restraint following from this consideration. The principle of "humanity" in international law on war assumes such commonalty. But even where there is no commonalty because of dissimilar cultures (as in the colonial wars of the past) or because it has been eroded by propaganda or ideology (World War II, the Cold War), concern for one's own noncombatants must necessarily still operate to restrain use of indiscriminate weapons in one's own territory; this is simply a matter of self-concern and common sense. Moreover, disregard of the rights of one's own noncombatants tends to erode any inhibition the enemy may have toward harming them directly and intentionally. Finally, restraint from direct, intentional harm to noncombatants may follow from fear of

reprisal. The ability to project destructive force over long distances is characteristic of modern war, so that national homelands are vulnerable even when the theater of war is far away. In effect, the noncombatant populations of contemporary belligerents are held hostage against the actions of their armed forces. This is a fundamental reason for concern about use of nuclear weapons in combat in Western Europe. But if escalation is expected to work this way, then concern over its occurrence should operate as a powerful restraint against the use of indiscriminate weapons in areas where noncombatants are located, whether in Western Europe or elsewhere.

2. In areas where noncombatants are not present, such as desert areas or at sea, escalation to the most powerful weapons available is inhibited by proportionality alone. Considerations of proportionality always operate to undergird discrimination. This means that even where noncombatant immunity does not have to be taken into account, a restraining factor rooted in moral value still remains. Historically, when the costs of war were relatively more obvious and immediately felt than they have been in the last century, considerations of proportionality may even have been the more powerful of the two moral limits of the just war tradition, in terms of their practical effect. When the means of war were limited, they could not be squandered in the service of inferior ends. But a subtle psychological relation between ends and means has contributed to the transformation of modern war toward greater destructiveness: if the means of war become less limited, then the ends to be served by war become the more grandiose. The thinking that has produced this result is fallacious at its very core; the ends of war are fundamentally the same as they have always been, and only the possible means have changed. As a result, the problem of contemporary warfare is exactly the opposite of that confronting, say, a European monarch in the classic historical period of limited warfare, the eighteenth century.[9] Then the question was how to marshall enough force to serve the ends desired; since there was too little force available for all the ends to be achieved,

some were put off or forgotten. This required a serious effort to prioritize the ends of war. Today, with the destructive potential of war virtually, in practical terms, unlimited, there has often arisen a tendency to think that all possible ends can be served by such means of force.[10] But the very magnitude of this destructive potential militates against resort to all that is possible—a strategic thermonuclear war. This leaves no choice but to return to the chore of prioritizing the ends that might be served in war and determining what are the upper limits of the use of force that may rationally be employed in serving some, if not all, these ends. As in the days of Frederick the Great, some of the desirable ends of statecraft and war must be postponed or forgotten entirely. But whereas Frederick was limited by what he could do with the means of force he had, contemporary use of military force in statecraft must be limited by a moral intentionality that has decided in advance what ends may properly be served by the types of force available and which of the available types of force may properly be used in the service of these ends.

3. When there is no other choice than to endanger noncombatants, they should be evacuated from the area of battle. This stands as a positive moral obligation, going beyond the negative one of permitting them to depart if they wish. Rather, the obligation to avoid direct, intentional harm to noncombatants creates the duty to remove noncombatants from areas where it is foreseeably and unavoidably impossible to avoid harming them. This amounts to a limited approval of the idea of free-fire zones, though it does not extend to the creation of such zones for mere convenience of the military commander or to allow the use of indiscriminate or disproportionate types of weapons that are not genuinely necessary. Military force exists, at bottom, for the service of noncombatants, since in time of peace all are noncombatants; the purpose of evacuating such persons from areas where they would be foreseeably and unavoidably harmed by the genuinely necessary means of war thus rests on an obligation *to them*. This is not the case when noncombatants are evacuated for any other rea-

son, and international law rightly sets curbs on the movement of civilians against their will.

4. Finally, in the last resort, foreseeable yet unavoidable harm to noncombatants in a battle area may be allowed in order to protect noncombatants in other geographic areas who would otherwise be put at menace or to protect values of equal or greater weight than harm to innocent persons by the use of indiscriminate means of war.[11] Morally this is the last resort, not something that is admitted farther up the scale of possible actions. Again, we need to approach the allowance of such harm from the perspective of the obligation to protect noncombatants from the destructiveness of war. The issue is thus not in first place one of making a decision on the ground of proportionate reasoning (a few must die here to save the many there). It is rather one of how to discharge the obligation to protect all noncombatants, both here and there, both in the area of battle and elsewhere in the theater of war, both in the theater of war and outside it. The problem is analogous to that of how to employ scarce life-saving medical technology, though the terms are reversed: the omission of action dooms the patient who needs the technology in order to continue living, while in war it is the commission of an action that brings almost certain suffering and death to noncombatants in the target area. But to argue that this difference makes the one action right and the other wrong is specious. In either case the results—undesirable and desirable—are foreseeable and unavoidable, and this is the critical point. Once the decision is made to act, considerations of proportionality come into play, just as they bear on any and all acts of war, but again the argument from proportionality takes second place. In order to decide whether to harm one innocent person rather than two or to save two rather than one, the decision must first have been taken that any innocents at all may be harmed—or saved. The difficulty of reaching this prior decision is the reason why this option of admitting foreseeable yet unavoidable harm to come to noncombatants must always be a last resort, chosen only in the attempt to serve competing values of equal or greater weight.

The Cruise Missile

The concept of the cruise missile is not a new one; the German V-1 "buzz bomb" of World War II was a primitive cruise missile; yet the contemporary versions of this type of weaponry differ technologically from those primitive buzz bombs in two important ways, a fact which carries the potential of changing warfare significantly. The growing sophistication and military utility of cruise missiles were illustrated graphically in the spring of 1982 when, during the Falklands conflict, a single Argentine Exocet missile armed with a conventional warhead sank a thoroughly modern British warship. In World War I, long-range naval artillery would have been used for this task; in World War II, the relevant technology was aerial bombing or air-launched torpedoes fired from carrier-based planes. In naval use cruise missiles have already largely supplanted the heavy, long-range artillery that represents the best achievement of an earlier military technology. At present a sharp debate is being carried on as to whether the contemporary version of World War II technology, the carrier and its fleet of airplanes, has not also been antiquated by the development of highly capable and relatively inexpensive cruise missiles. In land warfare cruise missiles are thus far less significant. Because the distances involved are shorter, artillery remains the weapon of choice for tactical support. Similarly, because air support of ground troops currently depends in part on visual observation, no cruise missile can do the job of piloted ground-support aircraft. But where strategic service is the issue, the story is quite different: while strategic cruise missiles have not at present replaced the ballistic missiles that make up the largest part of the strategic force, they appear to have every potential of doing so. The moral implications of these changes in warfare, actual and potential, are our concern here, and in thinking about these implications we must, as with the neutron warhead, proceed by way of comparison with what has gone before.

Along with the technological sophistication that separates the contemporary generation of cruise missiles from the buzz bombs of World War II are two significant moral differences: the accuracy of the new weapons and the variety of types of warheads available for them. These characteristics also mark off contemporary cruise missiles from the weapons systems they most effectively substitute for: artillery fire and strategic aerial bombing.

Accuracy The World War II missile killed indiscriminately where it fell, and the place of impact could be controlled only by the vector heading on which it flew and the amount of fuel it carried. Thus it could hit only very large targets—those the size of a metropolitan area. British population centers, like London and its environs, were the chosen targets of the V-1. Its development must be understood in the immediate context of counterpopulation bombing by both Axis and Allies during World War II, and the corresponding erosion of respect for the immunity of noncombatants. The buzz bomb campaign against Britain was simultaneously a measure of psychological warfare against the British population to undermine support for the war effort and a measure of retaliation for the Allied bombing of German cities, just as this Allied bombing was itself a response to earlier German counterpopulation bombing of Britain and an effort to undermine civilian morale. The V-1 was a counterpopulation weapon in both intention and actual use; its inaccuracy kept it from being anything else.

Contemporary cruise missiles are, however, extremely accurate, being controlled by internal guidance systems and electronic sensing mechanisms rather than by flight vector and fuel. The earlier mode of aiming was in principle not different from the way one aims a thrown rock; the new mode allows for changes of direction in flight and "homing in" on the most vital part of a target by corrections of course close to time of impact, with the full potential of such controllability depending on the sophistication of the guidance mechanism. It would be, of course, possible to use these weapons against population centers, but because of their accuracy they could be limited to attacks on enemy missile-launching areas, military installations, concentrations of troops, and other targets directly related to the capability of

an enemy to prosecute the war. Herein lies the moral difference from the earlier weapon and, to a lesser extent, from
alternative contemporary weapons systems. Use against
military targets would be discriminate, avoiding direct, intentional, and foreseeable harm to noncombatants, their
property, and the civilization of the enemy nation generally,
as opposed to the moral indiscriminacy of the V-1, whose
chief aim was to kill noncombatants, destroy noncombatant
property, and disrupt civilian life as much as possible, with
military damage only an incidental possibility.

In the same way, the cruise missile can in principle be
distinguished from current strategic warhead delivery systems, whose limitations remain a powerful argument for
counterpopulation strategies such as mutual assured destruction (MAD). Together with its relative cheapness and its
potential for avoiding detection in flight—which enable it to
reach an intended target—the accuracy of the cruise missile
could make possible for the first time since the thermonuclear arms race began a defense strategy oriented principally around the concept of counterforce warfare (where the
term *counterforce* is understood as including not only the
enemy's strategic nuclear force but military forces of all
kinds). From the moral standpoint this would be a step of
the utmost importance. The "balance of terror" concept present in the MAD strategy requires either that counterpopulation warfare be intended and, in event of war, actually
waged or that it be intended for deterrence only but never to
be used, thus amounting to a massive—and potentially disastrous—bluff. However understood, the counterpopulation
threat present here is extremely difficult to justify in moral
terms. We will look more closely at this problem in the following chapter. In the present context, though, it is useful to
note that the characteristics of the cruise missile open up
strategic possibilities that may be significant.

If noncombatant immunity (or, in other words, the moral
principle of discrimination) is to be taken seriously in our
thinking about war, the cruise missile represents a definite
positive development in weapons systems. After nearly a
generation of strategic thought that never strayed far from

the idea of direct attacks on enemy population centers, the cruise missile opens up the possibility of devising a strategy based on attacks that are aimed not at destroying large numbers of civilians but at neutralizing the enemy's military power—which is, after all, the legitimate aim of war.

Warheads The V-1 of World War II was armed only with conventional high explosive—though had the German program to develop the atomic bomb succeeded, it might also have been the first nuclear missile. But even without an atomic warhead the nature of this weapon would have remained the same: a counterpopulation device whose technical limitations fitted its mission of direct destruction of noncombatant persons and property. The contemporary generation of cruise missiles, as already argued, is a different sort of weapon altogether, one whose capabilities allow targeting directly against enemy military power. The nature of the warheads that can be used for arming the new missiles underscores this difference.

1. High-yield strategic nuclear warheads. The cruise missile differs morally from other current strategic nuclear delivery systems only in its accuracy and its ability to penetrate defenses. By comparison with the most advanced land-based ballistic missiles, these advantages dissolve, but a new one arises: the cruise missile represents a much less costly strategic delivery system than, for example, the MX. The same moral problem exists for the cruise missile in strategic uses as for current delivery systems, mitigated only by the factor of accuracy and its ability to reach the intended target. The fact remains that when this target is close to a population center, the very power of existing strategic warheads implies heavy destruction in nearby noncombatant areas. But the mitigating factors are nonetheless important, since they suggest that fewer strategic warheads may be necessary to destroy a given military target, such as a hardened underground missile silo. As a result, the total destruction in the area surrounding the intended target would be lowered. Morally as well as militarily this represents no mean advantage.

2. Low-yield tactical nuclear warheads. Current delivery

systems of such warheads are already both precise and difficult to defend against; such weapons are, moreover, meant
to be employed against enemy military forces, not against
noncombatants. So the advantages proffered by the cruise
missile seem already to have been reached in the tactical
nuclear realm. Indeed, from one perspective the cruise missile seems to offer a definite *dis*advantage as regards the
limitation of war. If deployed for tactical use, it could extend
the theater of operations so far beyond the area of actual
fighting by troops as to raise substantially the level of destruction to combatant and noncombatant alike. Yet the
ability of cruise missiles armed with warheads of the tactical type to reach staging areas, arsenals, strategic bases, and
so on might also reduce the need for directing large strategic
warheads at such military targets, with the possibility of
lowering total intended and collateral destruction. Indeed, if
the full potential of the cruise missile is realized, lower-yield
warheads may do the job it now requires a high-yield warhead to perform.

3. Conventional high-explosive warheads. The capability
of contemporary cruise missiles to discriminate among targets at long range appears to open up the possibility of replacing nuclear warheads with conventional high explosives
for tactical and even some strategic use. The V-1, militarily
speaking, was a poor retaliatory answer to the obliteration
bombing of German cities because of the limited destructive
power of its warhead. But morally this limited radius of
harm was an advantage; it remains so. Generally speaking,
the moral advantage lies with highly controllable weapons
of limited destructiveness and little redundancy of destructive power. The cruise missile armed with an appropriate
conventional warhead appears to approach this moral goal
quite closely in terms of its technical characteristics; what
remains necessary is the intention, expressed in tactical and
strategic plans and decisions during battle, to serve this
same goal.

After war is done everyone is a noncombatant, and nuclear war because of its long-term effects represents an inherent violation of noncombatant immunity. If cruise mis-

siles, because of their cheapness, their accuracy, their ability to penetrate defenses, and their ease of utilization in combat can be credibly armed with conventional high explosive rather than with nuclear warheads, this would be a desirable step backwards—back onto the path that leads to one of the most ancient principles in Western moral tradition on the restraint of war: the need to avoid wartime destruction that persists in its effects long after the war itself has ended.[12]

Conclusion

Much of the contemporary moral criticism directed against war focuses on the weapons available for use. Such concern is important, but unless the weapons of war are to be regarded as somehow like natural forces of destruction, representing the threat of primordial chaos in the same way as does the eruption of a volcano or the flooding of a river basin, such concern is not enough. Contemporary weapons are capable of such destruction, to be sure; yet the better focus for moral concern is upon the values and intentionality that guide weapons research, the deployment and intended uses of existing arms, the training and socialization of military personnel, and the overall framework of national policy within which war may be an unhappy choice. Contemporary weapons have no corner on the market for horror; to this the victims of all the wars of history would testify. The moral problem in contemporary war is the same as it has been in wars of the past: to hold the destructive potential in check, to make sure the use of force serves to protect and save values rather than destroying all that it touches. A Carthaginian peace is no true answer to the need for preserving what is of value. But the lesson of restraint and intentional moral control over the means of war is disregarded in advance when the model is one of uncontrollable chaos, as it is with Fussell, or of historical inevitability, as Mandelbaum's three revolutions suggest. The destructive potential of contemporary weapons should rather provide incentive to make human control over them the more positive and the more deeply informed by an understanding of moral value.

In the short run, the acquisition of such control requires giving careful attention to how the arms available may best—in the moral sense—be employed, and this carries implications for the entire sweep of military issues—particularly for tactics, socialization and training of officers and enlisted personnel, and formulation of military policy. In the longer run, it points toward the development of more manageable, more discriminating, and more proportionate weapons for use in situations where force is genuinely necessary. In the still longer run, humanity may hope for the establishment of effective means of removing conflicts or settling them without recourse to force. All these goals require our attention simultaneously; we may not concentrate on any one without attending to the others. But if we are to reach the long run, we especially must not allow ourselves to neglect the immediate prospect. For the weapons of war as for other human creations, we must manage what we have brought into being.

6

Strategic Targeting

The Historical Legacy of Strategic Targeting

The age of nuclear weapons dawned at the end of a war in which strategic aerial bombing of enemy population centers had become a routine, if not entirely uncontroversial, practice. By contrast with earlier forms of war, in which noncombatant immunity had been a generally accepted ideal, and in contradiction to the Hague convention prohibiting aerial attacks on undefended civilian structures,[1] the "total war" concept fused noncombatants with combatants as "the enemy," and counterpopulation attacks were represented to be a legitimate way of "carrying the war home" to undermine morale and concrete support for the war on what had already in World War I come to be called the "home front." The developments that brought this state of affairs into being were many and complex. I will mention four major factors.

First, the idea of total war itself, while at least as old as the Bible and no doubt even more ancient, has its more recent ideological roots in the structural changes that reshaped war in the time of Napoleon.[2] The wars of the ancien régime had involved monarchs and their relatively small armies of professionals and mercenaries; beginning with the French Revolution the entire nation was cast as simultane-

129

ously the cause for which to fight, the source of volunteer or conscript manpower, and the base of support for the military effort. With the industrial revolution the changes begun here were intensified, and the military and civilian sectors became yet further intermixed. In this coming together of two areas of life that had earlier been separate lies one of the roots of the idea that the enemy against which war is fought includes combatants and noncombatants alike.

A second stream leading to the strategic bombing of World War II was one of debate over doctrine—specifically, what purpose was to be served in war by air forces.[3] Were they to operate in support of land and sea forces, performing observation duties, acting as "spotters" for artillery, perhaps providing close support of troops by strafing and local bombing? Or was air power to take a more independent role, capitalizing on its mobility, range, and difficulty to defend against to strike behind battle lines, replacing artillery with bombs targeted much farther into enemy territory than any gun could reach? The first line of argument produced a concept that came to be known as *tactical* air power, while the second came to be termed *strategic*. These terms and concepts, with their respective doctrines, remain in force today. But the debate was more complex than this, for among the supporters of the strategic concept of air power some argued for its use against military staging areas, transportation centers, munitions factories, shipyards, and the like, while others argued for less discrimination, choosing among a spectrum of possible targets from the purely military to the purely noncombatant civilian on the basis of what might be judged best at the time.[4] This latter branch of the debate produced counterpopulation strategic bombing, while the former led to counterforce use of strategic air power.

The third major stream that nourished World War II counterpopulation bombing practices was technological. Simply put, neither the Germans nor the British at the beginning of the war had the technological capability to deliver bombers from long distances over appropriately military targets in close proximity to population centers, and even if they succeeded at this, their bombsights were insufficiently accurate to allow hitting the real target from the high altitudes at which the bombers flew for their own safety.[5] Quite apart from the intention to attack civilian morale—which was certainly present in the German blitz as well as in the British bombing of German population areas—these factors would have made counterforce strategic bombing all but impossible, so that once the decision was taken to pursue a strategic bombing policy, counterpopulation attacks were all that was technologically possible.

Finally, there was the factor of rage: Hitler's rage at the treatment of Germany after World War I, Churchill's rage at the German air blitz aimed at British cities, and later American rage at Japan for its attack on Pearl Harbor and its atrocious treatment of American prisoners of war. Because of this rage, counterpopulation bombing carried a genuinely punitive cast all through the war.

Such was the legacy, in brief, out of which the strategic countercity bombing practices of World War II arose; the use of the atomic bomb was no different, except in the magnitude of destruction it caused, from the conventional aerial bombing of London, Hamburg, Tokyo, and many other population centers on both sides in the war.

Do we remain the prisoners of this legacy? This is a question of the utmost importance for our thinking about the problem of war today. The strategic nuclear policy developed over four decades since Hiroshima has without question been shaped by the formative forces from the past that have been identified here. Unless there is cause to think that historical events have now carried us beyond this inheritance or that we now possess the mental, emotional, and political strengths to reject it, there is no point in considering alternatives to a strategic nuclear policy that directly and intentionally threatens targets in or near centers of noncombatant population, and possibly even these population centers themselves, in the name of deterrence but with the potential of carrying through on the threat in event of war. The causative forces that have shaped military policy up to the present remain importantly with us; so too the debates that have raged in the past continue to shape present dialogue; and mutual distrust based in systemic and ideological differences between East and West has taken the place of the emotions that produced counterpopulation war in World War II. So at first glance the answer to our question is that we remain very much shaped by the legacy that produced counterpopulation warfare in the first place. Yet mitigating factors weaken the hold this past has upon current and future policy, and these deserve to be raised to view.

In the first place, while a considerable intermixing of the civilian with the military undoubtedly has occurred as a result of the Napoleonic and industrial revolutions, it remains possible still to conceive of noncombatant status as genuinely different from the status of combatant and, even more important, to treat these two kinds of persons differently under the conditions of war.[6] A proportionately larger number of civilians than in earlier ages may be working in munitions factories, providing transportation services, sewing military uniforms, manufacturing other items that have a military use in a contemporary military force; whether the proportion of such persons is really larger or not does not matter because the point is that the sorts of work done in such capacities as these have throughout history put some civilians at risk during wartime, without simultaneously dissolving the status of noncombatancy held by others. The test of combatancy is today, as it was in previous eras, how directly one is engaged in supporting military activity. Thus in recalling his experience in the Thirty Years War one military participant noted with some reticence but a certain finality that women engaged in digging earthworks for defense had to be warned off, since such labor would lose them their privileges of noncombatancy; yet not all women lost noncombatant status because some dug trenches for soldiers.[7] Similarly, it is wrong to argue that if during World War II a Hamburg civilian dockworker was not immune from attack while working at his job, neither was his wife who prepared his lunch before he went off to work. Likewise it is wrong to argue that in a society where there is conscription a schoolboy may legitimately be attacked because the following year, when he is eighteen, he will be drafted and become a soldier. To argue against such blanket extension of combatancy over all inhabitants of a belligerent nation is simply to apply the principle used in the book of Ezekiel: "The soul that sins shall die. The son shall not suffer for the iniquity of the father, nor the father suffer for the iniquity of the son; the righteousness of the righteous shall be upon himself, and the wickedness of the wicked shall be upon himself" (Ezekiel 18 : 20). The wisdom voiced here is simply a fundamental principle of justice. No one can deny that the circumstances of war sometimes put legitimate noncombatants at risk; yet the principle of noncombatant immunity is not made null and void by this. Rather this principle sets up a standard: noncombatants are not to be the object of intentional and direct attack upon them as persons or as a class, and so far as possible noncombatants are to be spared the harm necessarily done in the course of war. The obligations implied here extend both to one's own population—not to endanger them by siting military or support facilities in the midst of large noncombatant populations—and to the populations of the enemy, who must live both with their government's decisions about where to locate military facilities and with the targeting policies of the other side.

The face of war has assuredly changed since the Napoleonic era made it a matter of the nation as a whole and since the industrial revolution so effectively intermixed the civilian with the military. Yet—and this is my fundamental point about these changes—we have tended to make more of them than they warrant. Human perception has moved beyond the actual developments here to assume a state of affairs that these developments do not constitute. It is simply absurd to regard all citizens of an enemy state as equally deserving of the risks of war; "the nation in arms" is a dangerous fallacy. By recognizing this fallacy we have the potential to reject that historical legacy which has taught us that counterpopulation warfare is legitimate in conflicts between nations, and thus to begin to retreat from the policies that shaped the conduct of World War II and that have been institutionalized in strategic nuclear deterrence policy.

In the second place, we must continue the reexamination

that has begun of the premises of the debate that eventuated in the establishment of strategic counterpopulation use of air power.[8] First, the public at large needs to become conscious, as scholars have been for some time, that there has in fact been a vigorous debate over strategic counterpopulation attacks. On the Allied side during World War II British authorities promoted such attacks, in opposition to an American policy framed around the concept that strategic bombing should focus on military and military-support targets. What is less known is that another debate was going on behind the scenes on each side; even as the opponents of counterpopulation warfare lost out to the bombing strategy of Churchill in Britain, so the American proponents of counterforce bombing in Europe eventually were overwhelmed by their opponents, both among the British authorities and internally, among the Americans who favored countercity strikes to attack German morale. In the war against Japan these latter forces held sway from the first, and there was never a concerted effort to hold the bombing of that country to counterforce levels. But technology aside (and more must be said about that below), nothing in the nature of the war against Germany and Japan necessitated counterpopulation bombing; the history of such bombing was a product of human intentionality, and it might have been otherwise. The course of the debate in the past does not any longer need to bind our future decisions; we are free, this time around, to reject counterpopulation strikes if we wish to do so.

Another feature of this necessary reexamination is that, under current conditions of war at least, the distinction between the concepts *tactical* and *strategic* sometimes disappears. As a result, policy must be framed to include both in a consistent way. I have already discussed this issue in the previous chapter in the context of nuclear weapons, and I will not repeat those arguments here. Instead, let us consider the difficulty of precision bombing with so-called tactical, or attack, aircraft in densely populated theaters of war, using two well-known contemporary examples. In its war with the Palestine Liberation Organization (PLO), Israel has from time to time directed aerial attacks against PLO head-

quarters in Beirut apartment blocks, and some of these attacks have accidentally hit noncombatants in nearby apartment blocks instead. Similarly, in air raids against North
Vietnamese factories, warehouses, and distribution centers
during the American involvement in Vietnam nearby houses,
schools, and hospitals were sometimes hit instead. Much
public outrage has attended such harm to noncombatants
(proving, incidentally, that the idea of noncombatant immunity is still very much alive), and persons should rightly be
concerned whenever something of this nature occurs. But
while it is moral and humane to care that noncombatants
should not be harmed by war, this does not mean that no
military force can be used against enemy combatants who
choose to shelter themselves among the noncombatant
population. The guilt for harming those noncombatants be-
longs first of all to their own forces, who illegitimately use
them as shields. The concept of precision use of force directed at the combatant behind the shield is a correct response to this. But even so, here we encounter the same
difficulty that is met when a strategic missile is targeted at a
military installation located in or near a population center.
It is not enough, morally, to lay the guilt on those who located the installation there and to accept the concept of collateral damage to noncombatants as if there is nothing more
to be done. Rather the obligation extends to attempting to
find other ways, less potentially destructive of the lives of
nearby noncombatants, to achieve the legitimate military
goal. Counterforce warfare, whether tactical or strategic,
thus runs up against the same obligations. The difference is
of the range and destructive power of the weapons employed, but the principles that should govern their use are
the same. This was not nearly so true in the early days of air
warfare, and the early debate accordingly drove toward a
sharp discrimination between tactical and strategic air
power. Now, though, the conditions of each type have begun
to merge, and what is said of the one must also be said of the
other. This means, as we think again about the possibility of
counterforce targeting as the limit beyond which war should
not reach, that small-scale tactical attacks in population

areas must be measured by the same yardstick that is applied to strategic missiles.

Reexamination of the third element in our strategic policy legacy from the past requires that we take account of the qualitative improvement in weapons technology since the end of World War II. Morally this means taking particular note of improvements in the accuracy of delivery systems and, for nuclear weapons, the development of less massively destructive warheads to replace larger ones. Let us first consider the former. Discrimination, one of the goals of a justly delimited boundary to the means of war, requires accuracy. In the preceding chapter contemporary cruise missiles were compared to the V-1 of World War II on this point; yet the same comparison distinguishes the kind of aerial bombing that was directed at population centers early in this war from that possible later, and the latter from what is possible now through the use of cruise and ballistic missiles. Similarly, early land-launched ballistic missiles and current submarine-launched ballistic missiles (SLBMs) suffer by comparison with the accuracy of contemporary cruise missiles and the land-launched Minuteman and MX ballistic missiles, while the SLBMs of the Trident system are expected to be capable of far closer targeting than the generation of SLBMs they will supplement or replace.[9] Reflecting back on the strategic bombing debates of World War II, we see clearly that one of the reasons the British position favored less discriminate bombing and the American position more discriminating attempts to target military and support installations was that technologically the British bombers and bombsights were not up to the standard required for the latter.[10] Without long-range fighter cover only the American B-17 Flying Fortress could withstand German air defense during a daylight bombing raid, and having daylight was important if discriminating targeting was to be attempted. (Even B-17s bombed in daylight only at great cost in planes and crews.) The British bombers, by contrast, required cover of darkness to avoid appalling losses during their bombing sorties. Further, the advanced Norden bombsight in the long-range, high-altitude American bombers was not installed in the older, smaller, less effective bombers possessed by the British and initially their only means of striking into the heart of Germany. If the British were to have a role in strategic bombing at all, then, not having the technology that made discriminating targeting possible, they had to bomb indiscriminately. This technological reason for indiscriminate bombing was easily reinforced by the other reasons, emotional and political, for counter-population bombing.

If we shift the focus now to the early years of the development of strategic nuclear power, we observe a similar kind of situation. On the one hand was the attitude inherited and well remembered from the recent war: that strategic bombing of the population centers of an enemy nation is a legitimate, necessary, and effective means of war. On the other was the fact that over the long intercontinental distances between the two global superpowers, available delivery systems were not capable of hitting targets smaller than medium-sized.[11] Quite apart from Cold War ideology, then, the doctrinal and technological reasons for a counterpopulation strategic policy were powerful arguments for developing the kind of nuclear force that in fact came into being. Now, though, we are in a situation where accuracy is much improved and strategic doctrine is once more open to debate, and counterpopulation strategy must no longer appear to be the foregone conclusion it was during the crucial formative period of the nuclear deterrent force.

Further support for the possibility of modifying strategic targeting away from counterpopulation warfare comes from the development toward smaller, lower-yield thermonuclear warheads whose radius of destruction is such as to make it reasonable to argue for attempts at discrimination even in the use of nuclear weaponry. Because of their greater accuracy, lower-yield weapons will do what only high-yield weapons can do when delivered with less accuracy; the rifle bullet, delivered on target, creates far less collateral damage than a shotgun blast in the direction of the target, though only perhaps a single pellet from the latter actually strikes the desired point. The arguments advanced in our discussion of the cruise missile and the neutron warhead in the previous chapter apply to strategic targeting as well, as was noted in that connection. The current historical situation is simply different from that which shaped strategic nuclear policy in the past, and differences make it realistically possible to move toward the goal of discrimination in strategic targeting.

Finally we must assess the importance of the factor of attitude toward the potential enemy, the factor which I termed "rage" in speaking of World II. During the period of the Cold War this attitude might better have been expressed, for the United States and the Soviet Union, as ideological enmity. That feeling born in ideological difference remains, but more prominent in recent debate has been a fear that strategic instability may come to pass. Since the nuclear deterrent has worked so well to keep war from breaking out directly between the two superpowers (assuming that this is the major reason no such war has occurred), then a move away from what has worked so well in the past may create a strategic instability that will lead to war. Rather than some form of hatred directed at the Russian people or at Communism, the support for counterpopulation strategy now present in American debate appears to arise in part from hatred of instability.[12] This is a considerable turnaround from what obtained earlier, and morally it poses quite different questions.

Models of Strategic Targeting: A Moral Critique

There are only two basic possibilities for strategic targeting: counterpopulation or counterforce. These alternatives correspond to the fundamental difference between noncombatants and combatants; accordingly, counterforce targeting is also sometimes termed *countercombatant* strategy.[13] Any "mixed" strategic policy, involving targeting of both combatants and noncombatants, ultimately reduces to one or the other; this is not a third basic possibility. Both noncombatants and combatants may be expected to be found in or near virtually any potential strategic target; yet there remains a real distinction between, for example, the bombing of a port facility that also, inevitably but not directly or intentionally, harms noncombatants in or near the port, and the bombing of a bedroom community near the port in order to undermine civilian morale—including that of some of the workers in the port.

Discriminating between the two kinds of cases requires acts of judgment; the cases are not always clear-cut. Yet many cases are obvious on the face of things, and even where there exists some ambiguity, the ideal of distinguishing between these two morally different kinds of strategic targeting remains. The fundamental moral obligation is to avoid direct and intentional attacks on noncombatants. But when massively destructive weapons are employed, the fact is that large-scale harm to noncombatants can be accurately foreknown if such weapons are detonated in or near a population center, and this knowledge must be included as one element in judging right or wrong intentions. If a member of a SWAT team were to fire a machine gun into a crowd of innocent persons in which a murderer has taken shelter, thereby killing and wounding a number of persons from the crowd, he would still bear moral responsibility for harming these innocent people though he might insist that his only intent had been to shoot the murderer. Whatever the machine gunner's frame of mind, his weapon was not one that could be used as an instrument of such an ostensibly good intention. The weapon of choice in such a situation, if we think in moral terms, would always have to be the least destructive and most accurate one. This might well include the sniper's rifle but not a machine gun, whatever the claim of the gunner. By extension, the use of outsize weapons against legitimate targets not only poses the moral problem of disproportion; it also raises the question whether discrimination was ever intended in the first place. This is a serious problem with strategic nuclear weapons. Accordingly, even when the ostensible target of a high-yield strategic warhead is a military installation on the outskirts of a city, one may question whether the use of a weapon with such a large radius of destructive force is intended only against the military base. Thus between the out-and-out intention to attack noncombatants directly for reasons of lowering morale, venting hatred or retaliating in kind and a highly restrained version of counterforce targeting in which targets in or near population centers are avoided, there is a large gray area, with some possibilities more resembling the one extreme and others more like the other. Since extremely few legitimate military targets are so isolated as not to endanger noncombatants collaterally, counterforce targeting strategy falls principally in this gray area, the area where moral choice must be exercised over each potential strategic target and over the level of force that may be used against it.

Within the two broad options of counterpopulation and counterforce strategic targeting there exist alternative forms these strategies may take. Counterpopulation strategy may envision an all-out exchange of thermonuclear weapons, or it may envision carefully selected and numerically limited, but still counterpopulation, use of some of these weapons.[14] Though the latter is proportionately better than the former—at least if it proves an effective strategy in the short run—both these versions of counterpopulation targeting are flawed by the fact that they represent a direct, intentional attack on noncombatants and are thus a violation of the principle of discrimination, or noncombatant immunity.

Can any circumstances be imagined in which this blanket condemnation of counterpopulation targeting would not apply? The first response must be that where an all-out nuclear attack is concerned, it is difficult or impossible to imagine it ever serving to protect or preserve value, given the value it would destroy. As we have argued already in chapter 2 above, this remains true whether the attack in question is preemptive, simultaneous, or retaliatory: in other words, here as elsewhere the *order* in which the force is employed does not dictate the moral issue; that depends on other factors entirely. Where the question has to do with limited counterpopulation strikes with strategic weapons, the moral importance of not acting directly and intentionally to harm noncombatants remains in first place. But as argued in the previous chapter for tactical and theater weapons, it is at least arguable that there may be times when in order to protect or save one group of noncombatants it is necessary to harm another group.[15] Even if one makes the decision to do this, the obligation remains to limit such necessary and justifiable harm so far as possible. A limited counterpopulation nuclear strike might perhaps fall within this severely limited sphere of exception to the blanket condemnation given above. Even such a limited strike, though, might very well exceed the bounds dictated by proportionality, and thus in practice the severest tests would have to be applied to justify this sort of action.

If we are to think of the possibility that strategic force may be morally permitted, it is counterforce warfare, and not counterpopulation strategy, that we should seriously examine. Such use of force is within the broad historical tradition of warfare that requires that it be between combatants; while noncombatant lives and values may be endangered when military forces are attacked, they are endangered only accidentally and not by design or claim of necessity. Thus the idea of counterforce warfare is an attempt to secure the possibility, however remote yet imaginable and potentially attainable, of achieving the ideal that noncombatants be spared the ravages of war.

In the contemporary context three related and overlapping but conceptually different kinds of counterforce strategic targets require attention: an enemy's own strategic nuclear force; military forces generally, including conventional as well as nuclear installations; and the command, communications, and control centers that would, in event of war, direct the use of enemy military power.[16]

Some moral advantage lies in the strategic targeting of a potential enemy's own nuclear striking force; yet there are also important disadvantages with this form of counterforce strategy. Positively, such targets are typically located in relatively uninhabited areas where the collateral loss in lives and values would be minimized. Further, such an attack would strike at the most formidable threat to one's own or allied noncombatant populations, thus perhaps diminishing this threat. But negatively, the difficulty of achieving the nearly total destruction of the enemy strategic force outweighs this advantage, and for greatest effect such a strike would have to be preemptive—thus representing an escalation in means of force used. A further serious moral drawback is the collateral damage that would be caused from the massive amounts of radioactive fallout that an attack of the requisite strength would create, even if there were no retaliatory response. This damage would affect friend, foe, and neutral alike indiscriminately. The ideal of noncombatant immunity would here be quite literally thrown to the winds that carried the fallout over the globe. Militarily, the effectiveness of a strike against strategic nuclear forces is limited by the problem that each installation not disabled would still represent an enormous force that could be used against one's own population centers. As a strategy for limiting harm to these centers of value, counterforce targeting of an enemy's strategic nuclear power is dubious; yet the protection and preservation of such value is the fundamental purpose of justified warfare. Nonetheless, this remains a better strategic option, in moral terms, than either form of counterpopulation targeting.

In these same terms, a strategy that includes all sorts of military installations among potential or actual targets should perhaps be preferred over one that targets the strategic nuclear force only. But this is the case only if such general counterforce targeting represents a lesser threat to noncombatants than targeting only an enemy's strategic nuclear force. Let us examine this possibility.

As noted earlier, the fallout danger from a counternuclear force attack would threaten noncombatants all over the earth. While all atmospheric nuclear explosions produce some fallout, the total amount of fallout produced in the blasts necessary to destroy a hardened missile silo would be large, in proportion to the size and number of warheads employed: two or more high-yield warheads. By contrast, other types of military installations represent much softer targets, vulnerable to single warheads of lower yield. If we do not limit ourselves to thinking only of noncombatants in the immediate vicinity of the blast—as we must not—then the option of strategic attack against a relatively vulnerable military base might well cause less harm to noncombatants than an effective strike against a remotely located missile silo.

Related to this is the further consideration that the total number of strategic warheads necessary to achieve the desired end might be lessened by this form of targeting. This possibility follows first from the relative softness of the targets involved and second, from the disruptive potential that might be produced by careful selection of targets and careful ordering of the priorities among targets.[17] The military principle of economy of force is directly related to the moral principles of discrimination and proportion, and here all three principles might well be served simultaneously. The conclusion of this line of reasoning is that strategic targeting that potentially includes all military forces of whatever sort is morally to be preferred to targeting of strategic nuclear forces only.

But more must be said. Working against such "counterforces" strategy is the fact that it targets not only missile silos, air bases, or submarines located in remote areas, but also military bases that are sometimes located in close proximity to noncombatant population centers. The difference may, indeed, be more apparent than real; not all strategic nuclear weapons are to be found in remote areas. Mobile, intermediate-range missiles capable of striking strategic targets can be moved at will among noncombatant population areas; airfields where planes capable of strategic nuclear bombing may be found are not systematically located in much remote areas; and submarine port facilities are generally surrounded by populated areas. But in any case general military facilities can as a rule be expected to be found closer to noncombatant centers than strategic nuclear installations will be, and this implies a greater risk to noncombatants to offset the lessened risk that follows from using fewer and smaller warheads. The problem is aggravated by the difficulty of telling the difference, in practice, between targeting a population center and targeting a nearby military base. We may judge this difficulty by putting ourselves in the place of the enemy: is there any practical difference between a counterforce nuclear strike against the naval installations at San Diego or at Philadelphia and a counter-population strike against those cities? If the attempt is to avoid harm to noncombatants, this form of counterforce targeting is not clearly superior to the targeting of an enemy's strategic nuclear forces. In one important respect, it is clearly inferior: the former would reduce the strategic retaliatory capability of the enemy, while the latter, in cases analogous to those of San Diego or Philadelphia, would invite a counterpopulation response from an undiminished strategic nuclear force.

The paradigm for moral limitation in war calls for employing the least force necessary, using it against forces of the enemy, and doing so in such a manner as to avoid directly and intentionally bringing harm to noncombatants. In the kind of counterforce targeting we have been discussing, where the whole range of the enemy's military forces is put at risk, we move toward satisfying the first two of these moral aims, but at some cost where the third goal is concerned. This broad form of counterforce targeting is no moral panacea. Under some circumstances, where potential harm to noncombatants is minimized by the ability to discriminate a military force from a nearby population, the ability to employ weapons of less destructive power means that this option is preferable. But in other cases, where the noncombatant population is not distinguishable from the military force, this preference evaporates. What ought to be learned from such considerations as these is that a morally informed human intentionality must finally guide the choice of all strategic targets, whatever their nature.

When we turn to the much more selective targeting involved in so-called decapitation strategy, which defines its targets as the command, control, and communications network of the military and political forces of a potential enemy, the moral judgments are somewhat clearer. Here we find the principle of economy of force, already important in the second form of counterforce targeting, carried to a new level. Are the moral goals of discrimination and proportion also enhanced? This is the crucial question for this form of counterforce targeting, and the prima facie answer must be that, ideally at least, here these three principles converge. Economy of force implies the use of the least amount of force necessary to achieve a desired objective; proportionality means suiting the degree of force used to the significance of the object, but it also suggests using the least force necessary, and thus it includes the idea of·economy of force. The general requirement of discrimination is avoidance of harm to noncombatants; more specifically, it means no direct, intentional, foreseeable damage to noncombatant lives, property, and associated values. Proportionality and discrimination do not always point toward the same action: preservation of noncombatant immunity, for example, may require the expenditure of more force—and perhaps more combatant lives—than would be the case if proportionality (or economy of force) were the only guide. But fundamentally the point of both these moral principles is to limit the destructiveness of war: proportionality by imposing restraints in general, and discrimination by marking off a particular arena for war and declaring it wrong to proceed against lives and values outside that arena. It is from within this fundamental congruence that decapitation strategy appears morally to be a worthwhile idea. By setting for itself even stricter limits than those posed by discrimination it builds what classical rabbinical thought calls a fence around those who should be protected, thereby strengthening the protection, and at the same time it implicitly requires lower levels of force—and hence destruction—than would a strategy gauged more broadly against an enemy's military forces generally.

In essence, decapitation strategy in contemporary form is a prolongation of the realization that without leadership a military force is powerless, and that without a particular political leadership in some instances the war would not be waged at all. Such strategy thus dictates that officers are to be preferred as targets over enlisted men on the battlefields, sergeants preferred targets over privates. It implies putting command posts and headquarters out of action and, frequently in past wars, capturing the capital city of an enemy nation and with it as much of the government machinery as possible. The principle involved is the same one established classically in international law that makes rulers liable for wars waged at their behest.[18] At the extreme, this principle suggests political assassination as the most discriminate and proportionate means of war; yet the difficulty of separating assassination from murder, which is universally taboo, has kept this extreme from being reached in the moral and legal traditions on war.[19]

In the realm of strategy involving the use of nuclear weaponry, the particular implications of decapitation change with the character of these weapons. Historically, decapitation has implied the use of the most discriminating and proportionate weapons: the individual soldier with his rifle looking for a preferred target during battle, the surgical artillery or air strike of the commando raid on a command post or base, the interdiction or capture of the capital city and enemy governmental machinery. But nuclear weaponry is something else again, tending to be both indiscriminate and disproportionate. As a result, in the end we are left where we were when thinking of counterpopulation strategy and the other forms of counterforce strategy: if decapitation means the use of a high-yield thermonuclear warhead targeted against an installation in or near a center of noncombatant population, it loses its moral advantage over the other forms of strategic targeting precisely insofar as it comes to resemble these other forms. Where, for example, the preferred target decided upon is the government of the Soviet Union, which has its own hardened underground shelters to protect it in event of war, the devastating effect of a nuclear strike on the other values encapsulated in the city of Moscow should also be taken into account. In the end, some aspects of decapitation strategy turn out not to differ significantly from other kinds of strategic targeting already discussed, especially insofar as actions against centers of command are concerned, for the high-yield nuclear warhead is a poor replacement for the more discriminating and proportionate methods that have historically been used against such centers. Does this mean that countercommand strategy may not morally make use of nuclear weapons? The answer is no. Rather it implies that the use of such weapons should be a genuinely last resort commensurate with the values to be served by this use, and this puts both this form of strategy and these kinds of weapons much lower on the list of priority than a prima facie consideration might suggest.

Apart from use of personal messengers or telephone wires—both of which have limited versatility in modern warfare—communication and control in the context of contemporary war implies the use of radio signals and satellite monitoring and transmissions. The radiation produced by an atmospheric nuclear blast creates a regional blackout in radio and satellite communications by disrupting the radio-wave signals. Such communications thus could not be depended on in event of a widespread nuclear war, and controls dependent on them would similarly fail. Such disruption would be a by-product of any of the other forms of strategic nuclear targeting already discussed; yet it could also be created in its own right by detonating nuclear warheads high in the atmosphere, well away from ground targets. The associated dangers would thus not be localized but widespread: they would include radioactive particles carried in the atmosphere, though not so many as would be created by a blast at or near ground level; a corresponding increase in the total load of radioactivity carried by the biosphere; the possibility of damage to the ion belts surrounding the earth that could cause long-term detrimental effects to life. Once again, the strategy is not so attractive as it looks at first glance; yet, comparatively speaking, the less it resembles the other forms of strategic targeting, the more preferable it is morally.

In the end, the best form of strategy, from a moral point of view, would be a decapitation strategy, but not one that relied on high-yield thermonuclear weaponry of the type currently strategically deployed. As pointed out earlier, historically decapitation has meant giving a premium to discrimination and proportionality in the practice of war, and this represents the goal toward which policy should aim. The replacement of high-yield warheads with lower-yield but more accurate ones would be a step in the desired direction, as would beyond this the replacement of nuclear warheads altogether by conventional high explosive. Some targets may have to be given up on altogether as requiring a level of force too great to be justifiable; this would certainly not be the first time such a course was taken in war. At the same time, though, other targets might well be singled out because of their vulnerability; this includes particularly military satellites, which for weight reasons can have little protection against conventional explosions nearby and even less against low-yield nuclear explosions farther away. Nor can they currently defend against high-power laser or particle beams, should these become feasible as weapons.

Conclusion

The final note, then, of this consideration of strategic targeting is that reasonable options exist to take us away from counterpopulation targeting toward a more morally defensible policy; yet at the same time these options should not be regarded as moral ends in themselves. Even the most restrained kind of counterforce targeting, decapitation strategy, is flawed when it relies on high-yield thermonuclear weapons of the current strategic type. Here, as we have found when looking at the problem of morality in contemporary war from the other perspectives discussed in this book, the direction to be taken is toward reducing reliance on such weaponry, and this, in turn, means two quite different efforts toward the same end.

On the one hand, as argued earlier in this chapter, we must try to forget the lessons of our immediate past which taught that war must be prosecuted to the limit of one's capacity, while remembering that the destructiveness of war has vastly increased over the last two generations. We do not have to be prisoners of this element in our past; war does not have to be fought this way. In rejecting this legacy from history, moreover, we become able to accept the far broader and deeper historical tradition that has been temporarily, but not totally, veiled—the tradition that teaches that war and the means of war must be justified and restrained by a concern to protect and preserve high values. This effort is thus aimed at recovering the moral identity shaped within our cultural history, and with it displacing the false consciousness that the unlimited warfare and ideological hatreds of the twentieth century have created.

The second effort aims forward rather than into the past, and it points toward the development of forms of weaponry, tactics, and strategy that can effectively replace the current ones, offering an equal or greater protection to the values worth protecting even by force while representing a lessened threat to these and other values. To say this is emphatically not the same as to embrace the notion, which is utterly false, that new weapons as such, particularly those that promise to shorten war, have a moral advantage over existing ones. To claim that they do is a dangerous idea as well as one that is at odds with history. The key must be to keep the development of new weapons, as well as the tactics, strategies, and policies that guide their deployment and potential use, in the service of a morally informed human intentionality. And this, in turn, points back to the creation in our contemporary world of a moral identity that understands what is of value and what is not, what deserves or requires to be protected by forceful means and what does not, and what limits even the justifiable use of force must observe. Thus the two efforts, the one looking into the past and the other into the future, are inextricably linked; together, they direct us away from those assumptions and practices in contemporary war that replace genuine value with ideology and restraint with unlimited destructive power, the twin evils of war in the contemporary age.

IV

Special Problems

7

Individual Decisions and Morality in War

The consciences of individuals are often strained by the circumstances of war. In this chapter we will examine two contexts of such stress, the issues of conscientious objection to military service and of disobedience to superior orders. The first of these has to do with the decision every individual must make whether to participate in a war or not; the second revolves around the kind of decision that few persons in fact may confront: what to do if ordered to act in an immoral manner. Only a comparatively few individuals have the responsibilities of framing policy or deciding on the course scientific research into weapons development should take, more persons—though still a comparatively small fraction of the population of a nation as a whole—exercise the moral responsibilities imposed by command; and at the far extreme, every citizen in a democratic society is charged with responsibility for helping to influence the shape of national politics and of the national military posture. In the space between the responsibilities of the few and those of the many we find those of the persons actually confronted with service in war, not as participants in the policy process or as citizens engaged in the political life of the national community but as bearers of arms; not as commanders (though some will command others) but as subordinates. This in-between space is the area in which is found conscientious objection, either to military service generally or to some particular aspect of it, including a specific order perceived as immoral. Thus in our thinking about morality and contemporary warfare, it is important that this sort of moral stress be addressed, both in general and in terms of the potentialities of contemporary warfare.

Conscientious Objection to Military Service: The Problem of the Individual's Entry into War

Responsibility and Function
The safety of the community is every citizen's responsibility. Historically this idea has typically meant, in the most general terms, that all persons not set apart because of their social function or their inability to bear arms could be called into military service. It is not accidental that these two tests, social function and ability to bear arms, have also traditionally been employed to determine who are worthy of protection as noncombatants. The correlate of having some persons who are obliged to give military service is having others who are not; accordingly, in time of war the logic of military action is to proceed against the former, who represent the genuine threat of force, rather than the latter, who are in principle set apart from this threat. The problem of conscientious objection to military service, whether by an individual or by a group, is thus linked to the broader problem of how to define the obligation of a citizen to help ensure the safety of his or her community, the reverse side of which is how to identify those who are the very ones within the community who are to be protected—the noncombatants. In taking himself out of the category of those obliged to perform military service a person makes himself, by definition, a noncombatant, and thereby imposes on those who do serve in the military an obligation to include him among the noncombatants whose lives and values they are pledged to defend. The problem, then, may not be narrowly reduced to one of an individual's decision to refuse military service;

rather, it is a question involving the community as a whole, the protectors as well as the protected. For by imposing an added burden on the former the conscientious objector gives them some say in deciding whether his claim to be exempt is valid; that is, the imposed obligation must be accepted. Similarly, by adding himself to the number of those to be protected the conscientious objector implicitly diminishes the share of protection each noncombatant may receive. That is, conscientious objection either increases the cost of legitimate military protection to the rest of society and particularly to those who may have to pay the cost with their lives, or else it reduces the amount of protection available for each noncombatant person or the other values worthy of defense. The conclusion of this reasoning is that the refusal of military service depends on the willingness and the ability of the community at large to tolerate such refusal while protecting other noncombatants and the values of the community at large.

Viewed in its totality, the question of conscientious objection may not properly be separated from the broader debate over what persons ought, by reason of their functioning in society, to be identified as noncombatants. The resolution of this debate must be formally like that reached in every new stage of its development in history: the community as a whole, acting as a moral entity, must define the scope of the obligation to bear arms, thus how far to go in defining the right to seek noncombatant status by reason of social function. Understood from this perspective the refusal of military service for reasons of conscience must be weighed against other values that compete with the value of protection of freedom of conscience. Or, in other words, claims of conscience cannot rightly be treated as moral absolutes, whatever one may think of the absoluteness of his own conscience. The moral and political traditions of our culture have recognized claims of conscience as representing a high value deserving of protection; yet it is one among other values, and these same moral and political traditions have limited the right of each individual to act as if his own conscience were absolute by taking account of the impact of such action on other persons. The right of freedom of conscience thus has bounds, and it is the role of the community at large to determine how much such freedom can be tolerated without endangering the community itself, which exists to protect such rights as this.

The claim to conscientious objection to military service is often made from a religious base, and thus it is helpful to consider how a position similar to the one I have sketched might be put in theological argument. The German theologian Helmut Thielicke advances such an argument in the midst of a detailed discussion of conscientious objection that is both politically insightful and theologically informed.[1] While Thielicke does not speak specifically to the American debate over conscientious objection, he does represent the broad moral tradition shared throughout Western culture, and thus his analysis is applicable to our present discussion.

Thielicke's position, summarized briefly, includes three main postulates: (1) Because of its duty to keep order and protect itself, the state has a right to demand military service from its citizens. (2) Because each citizen has both a moral and a political existence, the citizen must accept the demand of the state. "He will take his stand," writes Thielicke, "not as a stateless individual, but as a responsible citizen, one engaged in that conflict which is inherent in the state and in the human existence which is bound to it." (p. 532) This may involve him in suffering. (3) The state ought to frame laws that minimize the suffering its citizens must undergo. In the present context, this implies some compromise on conscientious objection, a compromise Thielicke describes as between the extremes of universal military service and an all-volunteer military. Speaking of the conflict between man's moral and political being, he writes:

If the conflict is inherent in democracy, and if in principle there can be no easy solution, this does not mean that the state is therefore justified in deciding on one of two radical alternatives: either an uncompromising insistence on universal military service and a complete suspension of the constitutional principle of freedom of conscience in this particular sphere, or the concession of unlimited play to the individual conscience and the practical introduction of completely voluntary military service. For in the case of the first alternative the state would be fanatically overlooking or violently setting aside the tension of values in which it is implicated. And in the second case it would in part be doing the same thing—challenging equality before the law and making the distribution of the burdens of the state dependent on the whim of the individual—and in part impairing its own capacity to function effectively as a state. (pp. 533–34)

If these "radical alternatives" are rejected, what positions are left to fill out Thielicke's "compromise"? The best answer to this question is to be found by considering the kinds of distinctions the state may make, according to Thielicke, in a law providing for conscientious objectors. First, two kinds of distinctions may *not* be made. The state may not distinguish between those who repudiate all war and those who reject "a specific war, or a specific mode of war, for example atomic war, on the basis of factual judgment; for both these decisions of conscience can have the same ethical rank." Nor may the state distinguish between "true objectors . . . and opportunists, cowards, and habitual dissenters . . . , for conscience is invisible." (p. 534) On both these counts even the most recent versions of American draft law appear immoral. For, as the 1971 landmark Supreme Court decision *Gillette v. United States*[2] has shown, the law did indeed discriminate between those who reject all war and those who reject only some wars. This implicitly gives a higher rank to the position of the general conscientious objector than to that of the selective objector. The distinction between what the law does say and what it should say is thus sharply drawn. Similarly, the law of the *Gillette* period did attempt to discern the "true objectors"; this was the intent of the clause requiring objection to be based in "religious training and belief"—even when that clause is broadened to include general pacifism individually arrived at.

Though he rejects these two possible distinctions that the law might try to make, Thielicke offers three possible "pragmatic" distinctions:

[T]he state can accept only those distinctions which (a) offer some guarantee that the motives underlying the objection are truly those of conscience, (b) are based upon a certain tangibility attaching to the decision of conscience, and (c) are so structured that they can apply only to a limited number of cases. (p. 534)

How a law may be framed which avoids the first two kinds of distinctions while embodying the last three is precisely what is at issue. And it must be said that Thielicke does not offer Americans any radically new conclusions. He suggests that exemption of Quakers, Mennonites, and Jehovah's Witnesses, as well as members of similar groups, is a rational aim for the state. These groups are highly visible; they reject war as a conclusion of a more general set of beliefs, their "comprehensive legacy of beliefs" makes it easy to spot "outsiders who come in for ulterior motives," and their members are willing to suffer for their beliefs. (pp. 535–36) In any case the state cannot fully achieve justice for all its citizens who conscientiously object to war; nor should it try. It should seek to be "only minimally and not maximally just." This follows from its character as an "emergency order between the fall and judgment." (p. 537)

It is difficult to perceive how a law granting conscientious objector status to members of peace churches and pacifist groups would avoid the distinctions which Thielicke himself has argued must be avoided. Much could be said here; I will make only two observations. First, exemption of members of groups such as Thielicke names seems an obvious violation of the principle that the state may not distinguish between objectors to all war and objectors to some wars. For the very visibility of such groups results from their objection to war in general. Second, that the nature of such groups makes it easy to spot "outsiders who come in for ulterior motives" seems a clear denial of the principle that no distinction may be made between "true objectors" and "opportunists, cowards, and habitual dissenters." Thielicke's example is as fraught with difficulties as recent American selective service law.

In spite of these glaring problems with applying the positive side of Thielicke's thought on conscientious objection— problems which might easily lead to the rejection of Thielicke for having nothing of wisdom to say to the matter under discussion—the general principles underlying his treatment of this issue are of considerable value for thinking it through. To summarize briefly again, they are three: (1) the state may demand military service; (2) the citizen must accept the state's demand, though the peculiar character of his acceptance may involve him in suffering; (3) the state should seek to minimize the suffering of its citizens. Taking these principles seriously means entering into the dialogue between the individual conscientious objector and the state, with the objector standing ready to suffer for his refusal to enter military service (an attitude of acceptance toward the state's legitimate demand on him), while the state seeks to reduce that suffering to the lowest level commensurate with justice—and Thielicke would add to the minimum consistent with order and the conscientious wish of the individual not to receive favored treatment. Though the example earlier cited from Thielicke does not go so far, these principles would appear to drive toward a law somewhere in the spectrum between recent draft law and the establishment of a service corps composed of military, various kinds of paramilitary organizations (for example, police, firefighting), and civilians. Ruled out on principle is the volunteer army, for it both rests the burden of protection of the state on the "whim of the individual" and, perhaps more important, is inherently less just than some form of the above because it does not challenge the conscience of every citizen equally.

Advice, Consent, and Dissent
Another avenue from moral tradition into the question of conscientious objection to military service is through a consideration of the role of each citizen to give advice within the political process of the community, to support the community by taking on the burdens of decisions made on its behalf, and to dissent responsibly from such decisions when he or she judges that they are wrong. Before the advent of democratic governments the full exercise of this role—and its accompanying responsibility—was limited to a relatively small number of persons close to the centers of knowledge and power within a society, and Western moral theory was

shaped around this model until the beginnings of the modern period. The theory regarding right behavior for citizens began to change with the writings of such men as Locke and Rousseau, and empirical practice was reshaped in its turn. What modern political theory essentially did in this matter was to extend the role of the few to the many, so that the rights and responsibilities of advice, consent, and dissent in principle were extended across the body of the electorate within a given polity. Accordingly, since the rise of democratically governed societies it has to be granted that all citizens have a share in this role to a greater or lesser extent, though the precise shape of each person's share depends on a great many factors.

One structural factor is that responsibility can never be removed from this role: the adviser must bear the burden of his advice, the dissenter the burden of his dissent. This is comparatively easy to see in practice in the close counselors of a medieval prince, all of whom typically stood to lose a great deal if their decisions produced bad results.[3] But the principle involved is both broader and deeper, and in the present context it means that the conscientious objector must not only avoid any appearance of seeking a "free ride"[4] but must also take responsibility for the impact of his decision on the remainder of the community.

Within this structural framework of the linking of right and responsibility other factors shape each citizen's share of the role of adviser in the community's decision-making process. Whatever their faults—and in many cases ambition or venality clouded their virtues—the close counselors of a monarch even through the nineteenth century and into the early twentieth could claim to have superior knowledge, experience, perhaps special training, and possibly superior ability reflected in achievement. Ideally the chief counselors of contemporary heads of state should have similar qualifications, all of which find expression in the ancient Greek idea of virtue. But comparatively few citizens are so equipped, and the transference of the role of advice, consent, and dissent from the few to the many in democratic theory and practice is rather the establishment of a high goal toward which all should strive than a statement of empirical fact about the equal merits of all persons as advisers. Rousseau's doubts in this matter led him to separate his idea of the "general will" from majority rule; Locke, by contrast, shaped a theory in which majority rule is held to be self-correcting toward the good of the community. Both traditions have helped to form modern Western societies, and both ideas are mixed in the shape of American public life. Little difficulty arises under either model when one agrees with the course taken in decisions made on the community's behalf, but the case of the conscientious objector is precisely one of not agreeing with one or more of these decisions. Here what must be said—we remain within the framework of linked right and responsibility established earlier—is that the objector has a special responsibility to approximate the qualifications of those to whom premodern political theory thought it right to reserve the role of advice, consent, and dissent: that is, the objector must be able to point to his own knowledge, training, experience, and perhaps superior ability to serve the community in other important ways than by military service.

These reflections imply that conscientious objectors to military service should constitute only a relatively small, specially characterized group within the community at large. Indeed, we must go further: if conscientious refusal of military service expands beyond these quite restricted boundaries, it may be a sign of the breakdown of that community as a unit or it may bear witness to a miscarriage in the political process. The widespread resistance to the American involvement in the Vietnam war exemplified both of these themes. It is not necessary to think of the most radical protesters, those who embraced programs of revolution and employed terrorist tactics in seeking their ends; more to the present point is the decision of a great many draft-eligible young men and, in some cases, their families to flee a society where they no longer felt at home and seek new lives in countries such as Canada and Sweden. If the actions of these people may be taken as exemplifying the breakdown of community, then those draft resisters who challenged the form or substance of existing draft law in the courts may be taken as examples of protesters who, while continuing to believe in the American political process as fundamentally sound, sought to correct what they perceived as a miscarriage in it. My point is the same in either case: if conscientious refusal of military service becomes a widespread matter, it should be taken as a sign that something has gone wrong in the policies for utilizing that military service, and a new balance should be sought.

Another implication of this line of thought based in the role of advice, consent, and dissent within a community is that conscientious objection ideally should always be selective. This is the same conclusion we have already reached in reflecting critically on Helmut Thielicke's argument, and if it broadens the category of potential conscientious objectors, it also implicitly makes the qualifications for such refusal of military service both more stringent and more in keeping with the moral values of just war tradition.

American selective service law, as it has taken shape from the time of World War I to the present, of course excludes in principle the possibility of such selective objection. It may be wondered, in this connection, whether the lobbying efforts of the various "peace churches" which helped to shape this law and its interpretation through various incarnations in fact shaped it in the right way. It may indeed be true that every Mennonite or Quaker subject to the military draft could pass the type of test that I have suggested is necessary (though membership in a religious group in no way proves that an individual shares fully the doctrinal teachings characteristic of that group); the greater difficulty arises when the tables are turned and the assumption is made that *only* members of such faiths may claim to be conscientious objectors or that, like the idealized "peace church" member, every conscientious objector must refuse service in all wars. *Gillette v. United States* eliminated the first assumption, but the second one remains. Its effect is to separate in principle those acts related to political dissent and those acts related to military service. It is not at all clear that this represents the juster option in law or reflects properly the moral traditions relevant to the matter of advice, consent, and dissent in the performance of political (including military) obligations.

Consider, for example, the curious fact that Catholics have in the past generally been denied conscientious objector status because they belong to a "just war" church and not a "peace" church. To be sure, the position that the individual believer and not the Church may declare the injustice of a particular war has not been much favored among Catholic moral theologians.[5] But nonetheless the problem is a serious one, and its implications extend beyond the membership of the Catholic Church. Should *any* person, Christian or not, who holds to the moral tradition that there are just and unjust wars have the right, as an individual, to distinguish between them? In the sixteenth century Franciscus de Victoria drew precisely that conclusion. In the case of his being called to participate in a war he considers unjust, Victoria argued, a citizen may refuse military service, but he must observe two conditions: he must have serious and weighty reasons for his judgment, and he must accept the right of the state to punish him for his refusal to serve.[6] This is consonant with the argument I have made, as well as with that of Thielicke. A further theological opinion to the same end is given by the influential Swiss Protestant dogmatist Karl Barth: all conscientious refusal to give military service, to be truly conscientious, must involve objection to a particular war. In Barth's context this idea follows from his description of the character of God's Word addressed to man and man's hearing it as Word—a call and response always set within some particular historical situation.[7] There would thus seem to be no common ground between Barth's position and a selective service law that honors only refusal to serve in *all* wars. Such refusal cannot by its very nature be conscientious, on Barth's terms. Not can it, I have suggested, in the terms of just war tradition considered broadly.

The conclusions implied by this and the previous section can be stated simply. First, the concept of conscientious objection to military service needs to be set fundamentally within a broader context of the individual's responsibility to serve the community, including giving protection to the community. The right to refuse military service on conscientious grounds is therefore one that only the community may grant, and it may set the conditions according to its genuine needs, while respecting the person of the individual conscientious objector. Second, the tests of conscientious objection should be placed within the framework of the role of advice, consent, and dissent in the decisions of the community, as these have been defined in the moral and political traditions in which we participate. This implies that refusal of military service is not legitimately separated from the role of political advising; it implies further that individual conscientious objectors must demonstrate by their knowledge, training, experience, and willingness to bear some other comparable social burden that they are acting within this framework in which right and responsibility are structurally linked. Third, whatever the administrative usefulness of legally allowing only refusal of service in all wars, a scrupulous effort should be made to redefine selective service law so as to base it on decisions involving particular wars. This might well in practice produce the same results, especially if the tests applied are framed with appropriate rigor and seriousness. But whatever the results, it is difficult to see that such a change would produce a law with effects any less just than the present one, which rewards the external signs of membership over the internal convictions of conscience.

Refusal To Obey Unjust Orders: A Problem in the Individual's Participation in War

Much of what has been argued above regarding conscientious refusal of military service also bears on the case of refusal to obey unjust orders. There it was argued that the individual's moral responsibility regarding participation in war is first of all to the community and not to himself. But responsibility toward the community is not identical with obedience to an order of a particular government; the values of the community itself always stand above such particulars. Only an individual can take responsibility, and the conscientious objector's claim is grounded in this realization of what it means to be a moral agent as well as in his conviction that the act of objection obeys a higher law than that of the governmental authority in question. But if this claim neglects the community, then the act in question places the individual agent implicitly outside that community as one who is not willing to be responsible for it and to it. When we move into the context of disobedience of superior orders by an individual in military service this fundamental framework remains. There is a right to refuse obedience in such a situation, as in the case of refusal of military service generally. Yet this right is not grounded purely in the individual's awareness of an abstract and inherently unverifiable claim of conscience; rather it is rooted in the same responsibility toward the community that led him in the first place to accept military service on behalf of that community. Thus the right is not inherent in the individual but is conferred by the community, and it is not an absolute right but one limited by constraints defined by responsibility to that community. It is characteristic of war, furthermore, that moral obligations and responsibilities often transcend the peculiar scope of the belligerents' vision; for this reason the Nuremberg trials, for example, could introduce the principle of crimes against humanity in spite of the absence of a previous definition of this idea in positive law, either domestic or international.

Thus obligations and responsibilities regarding war are focused in three locales: in the individual's own moral identity, in the values represented by the national community, and in the broader and sometimes less concretely known values of the larger community represented by the idea of humanity. These three foci constrain and limit one another, but they also provide mutual support and enhancement. The interaction among them presents us with two quite different sorts of cases involving disobedience to superior orders.

The Individual's Decision vs. the Values of Community
An individual's concept of what is an order he ought not morally to obey may not correspond to the collective wis-

dom expressed through the values of the larger communities in which he participates, and in such a case other members of these communities have a right to press him to obey and to call him to account for disobeying. As in the case of conscientious refusal of military service, it is the role of the national community to define through its domestic law how far such disobedience can be tolerated and how it should be punished.

In the case of disobedience of orders, military regulations represent the legal vehicle through which community pressure is generally applied, and the court-martial is the particular context in which the decision for or against toleration, for or against specific punishments, is made. Ideally this should provide as appropriate a means for expressing the community's sanctions as any other, but the history of military justice, fundamentally shaped by the problem of disobedience for other than conscientious reasons, makes it empirically poorly equipped to try cases involving conscientious disobedience of orders. The *Swedish Discipline* of the army of Gustavus Adolphus during the Thirty Years War,[8] one of the classic early modern military manuals and one of the sources through which to read the development of just war tradition, was in many ways a document aimed at ensuring moral conduct, though its principal focus was on keeping good order and discipline among the Swedish troops. Thus when it prohibited the looting of churches or the pillaging of civilians it reinforced the traditional moral limits set in the *jus in bello,* but it also ensured that the soldiers would remain in ranks and under the control of their superiors in case they should be needed for military action. This same dual thrust marks military manuals to the present day. The assumption here is that the interest of the individual soldier is essentially self-centered, and that it is the place of the community—here expressed through military discipline—to ensure a minimum of moral conduct at the same time that it ensures an effective fighting force. As a result, military justice has often been of a summary nature. In the battle order of Frederick the Great the officers were placed in front, where they could provide an example of leadership and bravery for their men; yet the post of the noncommissioned officers was to the rear of the line of battle, where their standing orders were to prod stragglers forward and to shoot any man who broke and attempted to flee from the battle. Similarly, Paul Fussell tells of a certain British officer during World War I who, encountering a group of forty British soldiers who were, in the midst of a general retreat, attempting to surrender to the Germans, shot thirty-eight of them on the spot to prevent their doing so. Explaining this action later, the officer emphasized the need for a "leader of sufficient courage and initiative" to check such weakness on the part of the troops to keep it from infecting the entire army.[9] The context of all these cases is the need to uphold discipline against the individual soldier's self-interested tendency to serve himself at the expense of others.

Where genuine conscientious disobedience to orders is concerned, however, the motivation rises in just the opposite way: not out of self-interest but out of concern for the values maintained by the larger community, and by which military life is bound along with all other elements within the whole. As in the case of conscientious refusal of military service, then, the test of genuineness in a claim to be disobeying orders out of conscience is whether the individual in question is willing to have his own self-interest suffer. This implies the threat of punishment; yet if the disobedience in question does in fact serve the community—that is, if to obey would harm the values expressive of that community— then actual punishment goes beyond justice. For this reason a system of public judgment rooted in the importance of maintaining discipline is not well adapted to judge the merits of cases involving the claim that disobedience of orders was for reasons of conscience. This implies that such cases ought to be tried not in military courts but in civilian, or at least in military courts under circumstances in which the historic preference for the maintenance of discipline has been structurally excluded by means of special statutes, regulations, or procedures.

None of this should imply that all claims of conscience

should be treated at face value. First, such a claim may be a mask for narrow self-interest, and where the specific interest of the individual in question cannot be easily separated from that of the larger community, it may be difficult also to determine when the individual is engaged in deception. Second, an appeal to conscience may represent allegiance to something the larger community does not itself value, or value in the same way as does the individual making the appeal. For an individual to refer his action of disobedience to superior orders to a political ideology not accepted within the community at large, for example, amounts to putting him at odds with his community. Even reference to religious values may not always deserve to be tolerated at face value by the community, because in a pluralistic society a diversity of religious views is to be expected, and the only way to ensure respect for all is to limit those particular expressions of one or another religious belief that tend to hurt persons and values outside that framework of belief. Finally, in third place, the individual who disobeys may simply be wrong: he may be making an appeal to conscience based on an erroneous or inadequate understanding of what conscience requires. The soldier who refuses to shoot a twelve-year-old guerilla armed with a machine gun on the grounds of the commandment, "Thou shalt not kill," or on grounds that children are generally to be treated as noncombatants is simply mistaken in his reading of what is the moral course in such a case.

For all these reasons, the claim to be disobeying an order for reasons of conscience must be treated, as in other cases involving a breach of military discipline or the breaking of a law, as an exception within the general public ordering of the community in question. This means the establishment of appropriate punishments, which may not in practice differ from those of disobedience for nonconscientious reasons, and the testing of conscientiously disobedient persons through appropriate and fair legal procedures. For his part, the individual who disobeys must be ready to bear punishment, even if he is personally convinced of the rightness of his action, because this is the most fundamental test of whether he has his own interest or that of the community at heart. But the community, for its part, should seek to give as much tolerance as possible to genuinely conscientious disobedience, in order to preserve and keep vital the value of service to higher principles even when a specific order or rule must be violated.

Conflict between National Purpose and Moral Values
The claim of national purpose is often, in war, made to excuse acts of military force that reach beyond the limits of what is moral. Such claims may not be legitimate in that they do not truly represent the values constitutive of the national community; yet in the context of war, with the full panoply of political and military pressure to sustain them, the situation is on its surface one of opposition between the nation's values and those of a higher, broader morality. If the individual acts on the basis of such a morality, he will find himself in conflict with the rules of his political and military superiors. This sort of case differs from the one treated above in two ways: the conflict may be more general and continuous rather than being something that is encountered only rarely, and then in special circumstances; and the judgment of the case cannot be carried on within the national community, which has been corrupted by the same wrong understanding of national purpose to which disobedience is directed, but must be rendered from outside, via war crimes trials. Because of this, the prior judgment of the international community as to what ought not to be done as an act of war is especially pertinent here (though it also bears on the first context for disobedience treated); the reason is that the values of this broader community implicitly include those of the nation-state in question, and thus what is agreed upon there stands in constant critique over against national policies. Specifically, then, this means that no individual ought to be held culpable for disobeying superior orders in order to obey generally accepted international conventions regarding war. Insofar as these conventions represent moral tradition on war—and they in fact constitute one of the major expressions of that moral tradition—attempts

by individuals to ensure the observance of the limits defined there express a properly grounded moral claim over against that of the sort of national purpose that rejects this broader pool of moral value.

Several problems, however, arise to interfere with the full exercise of the right implicitly granted here. First, there is nothing comparable to the system of justice presupposed in the previous case to ensure fair treatment of the individual who out of conscience disobeys a superior's order. The threat of a war crimes trial is much more remote than the immediate sanctions the state can impose, and so the prospect of ultimate justification in such a trial is extremely unlikely to help the individual at all in the short run, when punishment is liable to be imposed. If an individual ought to be ready to accept punishment in case he acted wrongly under the conditions of the first case discussed, here he should be resigned to receiving it, for there is little to prevent the state from utterly disregarding his claim to conscience.

Second, the individual in such a case as this is typically not in a good position to assess the motives or goals expressed in the national purpose, nor the moral or immoral implications of a direct order given him by a military superior. The kind of case in which the national order deviates from broader moral norms is generally represented by totalitarian societies, where ideological education attempts to represent the state (or the party) as the locus of the highest values, moral or otherwise. In such a framework of judgment, international conventions are made to fit the requirements of national purpose, and not vice versa. Realistically speaking, an individual socialized in such a system as this has little if anything on which to base a critical conscientious resistance to the system or a concrete act of conscientious disobedience of an order. It is further unlikely that such an individual will be enough in touch with the traditions of morality preserved in the larger culture to know what they require; rather, they will be mediated through the channels provided by the ideology of the national purpose. In the Nazi war crimes, for example, a typical excuse offered was that the accused had a duty to follow orders and had no way of judging the rightness or wrongness of those orders. Specious as this argument may have been in most of the instances where it was offered, the reverse side of it is that in societies like that of Nazi Germany or contemporary totalitarian states there is little opportunity for common soldiers to reach beyond what they are told. Here, then, conscientious refusal to obey orders may reflect more the individual's private perceptions of right and wrong, limited as they may be by the ideological constrictions imposed by the state, and not any real awareness of the claims of a higher moral community that itself stands in implicit judgment over his state.

Third, the specific formulations of international law as to what moral behavior requires may not themselves always adequately reflect the truly moral. Thus, for example, the face value of contemporary international law is that first recourse to use of force in conflicts among nations is wrong, that the only justified use of force is in defense against forceful aggression already begun.[10] An individual following this lead might very well refuse to obey an order to participate in a first strike, even in the face of undoubted provocation and imminent danger, claiming that to do so would bring him and the nation into violation of a moral order higher than the state. But in fact it is this particular element in contemporary international law that represents a deviation from the just war tradition; in that tradition the moral onus is on unjust aggression by any means, not on the use of weapons as such, which is only one way in which one nation may threaten another.

Fourth, and related to this, there are times in which, as argued earlier in the discussion of contemporary means of war, it is allowable, because of a conflict of values, to do what is generally prohibited. In the specific case discussed there, extreme circumstances may arise in which two separate groups of noncombatants may not simultaneously be protected, and in such a case harming one of the groups may be necessary out of respect for the principle of noncombatant immunity, not in violation of it. In this kind of case even the soldier of a totalitarian nation with an ideologically warped sense of national purpose would not be justified in claiming conscience for refusing to participate in such harm. At the same time, though, the difficulty of judging when such an extreme necessity is present argues for tolerance of such an individual judgment by the state and by military superiors.

Conclusion

Conscientious objection to military service and conscientious refusal to obey superior orders in military service are essentially similar moral problems, and what can be said about the one bears directly on the other as well. This brief discussion is more an attempt to lay out an overall perspective on what is at stake than an effort to treat either problem in any detail. That selective conscientious objection to military service, as treated here, is morally preferable to universal rejection of such service draws this kind of individual moral action closer to the act of refusing to obey orders on moral grounds. Similar kinds of rights and responsibilities exist in both cases, and the sanctions of the community, including the tests for genuine conscientiousness and the possibilities for punishment or tolerance, should be framed similarly. But there is a difference: conscientious objection to military service involves a judgment as to the presence of a *jus ad bellum*, a justification for the waging of war, while conscientious disobedience of orders involves a judgment as to whether the orders as given violate the *jus in bello*, the requirements of justice and restraint in war. A person who has doubts about the latter should not refuse service, but he may rightly refuse to participate in specific wrong acts of force, even in direct violation of orders. Doing so may require more courage and conviction than conscientious objection aimed at keeping oneself out of the war, but at the same time it has the potential to help make sure the prosecution of an otherwise justified goal is carried forward through justified means. This was a notable problem in the case of the Vietnam war resistance movement: it was never clear, overall, whether the objection was to the reasons for United

States military presence there or to the means used to fight the war, and likewise with individual resisters to the draft it was often unclear whether service to the community—a protest against a war contrary to American ideals—was intended or a self-centered service of the individual resister's interests—that is, an unwillingness to take the risks of war himself. The first kind of dissent deserves to be honored, though whether it must be finally accepted and acted on by the community must be decided in each case anew. But the latter kind of dissent really has no moral foundation. Potential conscientious dissenters, as well as the community at large, should therefore take pains to keep these two kinds of possibilities scrupulously separated.

8

The Causes of War and the Restraint of War

This book has thus far focused on moral issues that arise when we think of the means by which contemporary war can and may be fought; in traditional terms, our discussion has been of the *jus in bello*. Most of the debate about morality and war that has taken place since the nuclear age began has been of this sort, with very little discussion indeed of the moral question that is logically prior: is the use of force in the service of political values in a particular situation justified or not? This is the question that has defined the part of just war tradition known as the *jus ad bellum*, and in the past it has received considerable attention at various stages in the development of Western moral thought on war. Moral discussion has concentrated on two aspects of the *jus ad bellum*, the requirement that there be a just cause and that there be a right intention behind the use of force. Legal contributions have focused instead on two other aspects, the requirements that a proper authority undertake the use of force and that this use be a last resort. Other elements in this part of just war tradition include the ideas that the destructiveness of war must not be out of proportion to the goods for which it is fought and that the purpose of the war be to achieve a better state of peace than would obtain otherwise. Both of these latter concepts have sometimes been treated by moralists in connection with right intention; generally, though, they have not been given the level of attention received by the first four concepts mentioned.

In recent debate moral analysis has simply ignored the two requirements that have traditionally engaged most moral thought: just cause and right intent. There has, indeed, been considerable discussion of the idea of proportionality, as a judgment that modern war is inherently disproportionate forms one of the bases of nuclear pacifism. But since the term *proportionality* is used in two senses in this debate, one to refer to the total calculus of goods and evils associated with a war and the other to refer to the particular good or evil of a given type of force in a war that is assumed already to be justified, it is not clear whether this judgment by nuclear pacifists refers to the former or to the latter. I suspect it carries both meanings in this context. In any case, proportion or disproportion must always be relative to something else, and to introduce this term throws us back upon the fundamental *jus ad bellum* issue, the question of just cause: what values may justifiably be protected or preserved by the use of force?

Putting the best face on the contemporary lack of discussion of this issue, I suggest that the participants in the debate have simply chosen to bracket it so as to deal with pressing questions posed by the rapid changes in warfare in the modern age. Beyond this, though, the positions in the debate have been sharply polarized over the question of whether values can be served by an all-out nuclear war, so that any middle ground has been difficult to claim.

Yet claim such ground we must, if we are to take seriously the reality of contemporary warfare, which presents infinite possibilities below the level of nuclear holocaust. Beneath this level the questions are the same as they have always been: when and how to protect what values by the use of force. In an atmosphere of polarized debate it is difficult to treat these questions seriously for fear of being perceived as occupying one or the other of the poles. Yet we may not continue to ignore them. The following treatment is meant to open discussion on the *jus ad bellum*, not to close it.

After an initial survey of positions, I move to a critique of a central idea in the contemporary *jus ad bellum*, defense, then turn to consider the issue of whether unlimited means of force may morally be used in a war known to be justified.

When Is Resort to War Justified?

Western moral tradition knows a variety of moral justifications for war. In the Talmud three types of justified war are identified from the Hebrew scriptures, with each succeeding type less morally obligatory than the one before: war commanded by God, an absolutely binding responsibility upon all; defensive war; and wars initiated by the king for some purpose of his.[1] Roman tradition insisted generally upon the presence of some wrong done, though this wrong might be defined variously: defense, retaking something lost, retaliation, or punishment. In addition Roman law and practice required something further: the authoritative publishing of the causes for war and a formal declaration that a state of war existed. The fetial priests performed these two functions, in addition to insuring via auguries that the gods approved—or at least did not disapprove—the plan to make war.[2] Augustine's view of war drew upon both Old Testament and Roman tradition, but with the addition of certain ideas from the New Testament. For him, as for the Talmudic scholars, war was just if it was commanded by God; such wars were those fought by Israel during the Exodus and the period of settlement in Canaan. Fighting purely in self-defense was, in Augustine's understanding, ruled out for the Christian by the need to follow the counsel of Jesus to turn the other cheek, but such restraint did not extend to letting the neighbor be assaulted or to turning the neighbor's cheek when he was struck on the one. Rather, as we have seen in the paradigm outlined in the introduction above, Augustine reasoned that defense of the neighbor against an assault in progress was not only permitted for Christians but required as a duty of love. When just war tradition coalesced as a coherent and consensual body of thought and practice during the Middle Ages all these influences were represented.

The framework of reasoning employed was fundamentally Roman, and at the core of medieval thought on justifying resort to war were the three Roman criteria: a war is just if fought in defense, in order to retake something wrongly taken, or in punishment for some fault already given.[3] But all these were given a characteristically Christian and medieval cast: defensive wars included those fought in defense of religion; the recovery of something lost included not only persons, property, and territory but religious rights; and punishment, under the pen of Thomas Aquinas, explicitly became the duty of the righteous ruler acting as "the minister of God to execute his wrath against the evildoer."[4] All these concepts, so modified to suit the spirit of the times, figured in the justifications offered for the medieval crusades. Apart from the conceptions of just war based on the Roman model, the Old Testament concept of war commanded by God surfaced in medieval disputes over whether the pope could, as Christ's vicar on earth, command a war in God's stead.[5] This issue was not finally laid to rest in the theory of just warfare until the dawn of the modern period, when Victoria baldly rejected religion as constituting one of the just causes for war.[6] But the religious wars of the sixteenth and seventeenth centuries followed anyway, and when Grotius reiterated this idea[7] it was only the general exhaustion of all Europe that caused it to win agreement the second time around. Still the issue is not truly dead, though, as twentieth-century experience shows. Besides the wars fought in our own time in which religious belief is at least one element offered in justification (examples include Northern Ireland and Iran), there is the matter of wars fought for reasons of political ideology, which functionally is a modern equivalent to religion. Like the holy wars of the past, ideological wars have proven hard to restrain, and for the same reason: when one's cause is absolute, it is easy to reason that the most extreme measures may be taken to defend it or to impress it upon others.[8]

International law in the twentieth century has gradually reduced the acceptable justifications of war to one: defense.[9] While a form of intervention is allowed through the acceptance of multinational agreements providing for mutual defense, Augustine's idea that it is a moral duty to protect the other who is being unjustly oppressed is not a part of the consciousness reflected in contemporary international law. But the concept of defense currently employed is an elastic one: it means not only the repelling of an injury in progress (the Roman and medieval meanings of the term), but reaction to aggressive action already taken and completed. For this reason the first use of force has increasingly been held up as the evil to be avoided above all: it is the fundamental form of aggression, the unforgivable act of hostility among nations.

Roman Catholic thought in the last century has moved along lines similar to those taken in international law. Describing the position of Pope Pius XII, John Courtney Murray noted that "all wars of aggression, whether just or unjust, fall under the ban of moral proscription," while "a defensive war to repress injustice is morally admissible both in principle and in fact." For Pius, aggression was equated with offensive use of force and was not a moral option.[10] John XXIII went somewhat further than either Pius or international law in ruling out any use of force to repair a "violation of justice" already accomplished, and this limitation has important implications for retaliatory strategic strikes.[11] John's successor, Paul VI, sounded a chord like that of the Kellogg-Briand Pact of 1928, the agreement aimed at outlawing war, when he declared before the United Nations, "Never again war!" But until that goal is reached he admitted the justice of defense—though not offensive use of force.[12] The American Catholic bishops have further emphasized the evil of offensive force by advocating, in their pastoral letter issued in 1982,[13] a renunciation of first use of nuclear weapons by the United States. The strength of this sentiment may be judged in part by the Reagan administration's response, which noted that the United States has renounced offensive war as such—a reference, though not explicit, to United States agreement to the Kellogg-Briand Pact and to the United Nations Charter.[14]

Catholic statements on morality and war, much more

than Protestant ones, have successively fueled public debate over the questions treated—perhaps because they are treated as authoritative teaching that is morally binding upon faithful Catholics. In fact these statements fall into the category of counsel rather than of obligatory requirements; yet the weight of a statement by a pope, by a highly respected church council like Vatican II, or by a nation's bishops acting in their national assembly must be granted to be considerable. The significance for Catholics of the American bishops' letter on war and peace must be weighed with this in mind; yet this letter, throughout its lengthy drafting process, became a focus for discussion and argumentation within the public arena generally.

Because of this latter fact, the opposition to the use of force found in this letter is worth probing further in the present context. In its second draft the letter explicitly praised nonviolence, raising pacifism to a level of equality with just war reasoning as an alternative Christian moral stance.[15] The position accorded nonviolent pacifism in Catholic history has not, though, been quite so simple or quite such a matter of equality with just war tradition. In fact, while (as this draft of the letter noted) many Christians of the first three or four centuries were pacifists, from the end of the fourth century forward the Christian tradition of nonviolent pacifism was carried almost exclusively by the members of religious orders, not by the faithful generally. This posture became part of the monk's vocation; it was not regarded as part of the vocation of ordinary Christians, for whom the use of force was permitted and spelled out with increasing exactness as just war thinking developed from the time of Augustine onward. The attempt of the second draft of the pastoral letter to give pacifism a place of equality beside that of just war tradition in Catholic teaching represented less an effort to be faithful to history than a recognition that pacifism is now embraced, in one form or another, by a significant and often highly energetic minority of American Catholics. Indeed, one of the members of the drafting committee, Bishop Thomas Gumbleton of Detroit, describes himself as a pacifist.

In the third and final drafts of the bishops' letter the emphasis is on reasoning from principles of just war tradition, with pacifism as an option for Christians given somewhat less prominence. Yet the option of nonviolence remains in the letter as a possibility to which all Christians, and not only monks and nuns, may find themselves called.[16] There is, moreover, in the final draft of the letter a recurrent theme of rejection of contemporary war that finds expression variously: in its citation of the judgment of Vatican II's *Pastoral Constitution* that war between the great powers would be "the almost complete reciprocal slaughter of one side by the other";[17] in its similar citation of the 1981 statement of The Pontifical Academy of Sciences;[18] in its highlighting of the theme of escalation and in its rejection of the possibility of limited nuclear war;[19] yet most obviously, perhaps, in its continued approval and development of the theme of nonviolence as connected to the idea of "peace" in a uniquely Christian sense.[20] Overall, the bishops' letter rejects violence not only in its nuclear form but with contemporary conventional weapons as well; it rejects not only counterpopulation targeting but also the idea of limited nuclear war; it rejects first use of nuclear weapons as well as any retaliatory second use "which would indiscriminately take many wholly innocent lives"; and it accepts strategic deterrence "as a step on the way toward a progressive disarmament," while rejecting the use of the forces that form the strategic deterrent: "severe doubts" are expressed about the development of "war-fighting capabilities."[21]

We have earlier noted that recent international law has increasingly hedged about the legitimate resort to force, establishing a *jus ad bellum* tied to the idea of defense. In the American Catholic bishops' pastoral letter the approach is different, being a development largely out of the just war categories of last resort and proportionality. In spite of adhering in principle to the idea that force may sometimes be necessary for the protection of values, this pastoral letter carries its argument against violence so far that it verges on the position that no use of force can under contemporary conditions serve justice or any other human value. In both of these cases we find resort to war as an instrument of national policy called into question and severely restricted.

Protestant moral thought is difficult to summarize because there is no single authoritative source for statements of consensus. One agency widely accepted as representing liberal Protestant opinion is the World Council of Churches, which has moved markedly in the direction of pacifism in the nuclear age. For practical purposes the voice of this organization has in fact become a pacifist voice, since its rejection of nuclear war is coupled with the assumption that contemporary war cannot be anything less than an all-out interchange of strategic nuclear weapons.[22] A supporting theme is the rejection of "militarism" as the evil opposing social and economic justice in the world. In this line of argument the service of justice is explicitly connected to non-"militarist" policies and practices, and Christians are called to "imagine ways to provide the establishment of justice for all as a means to replace reliance upon arms."[23] Such ways to provide for justice are necessary, since the goal is general and total disarmament of the nations of the world.

The World Council is, of course, not the only source for contemporary liberal Protestant opinion, and its constituent churches are not representative of the whole breadth of Protestant thinking on war and peace today. Some Protestant statements, like that of the Evangelical Church in Germany,[24] hold to the position staked out in international law that defense, even including reaction against an aggressive use of force already completed, is sufficient moral justification for war. Other Protestant bodies and individual persons range largely between these positions, though there are clearly positions that are more extreme than that of the World Council and that of the German Evangelical Church. Among individuals, Paul Ramsey is the Protestant who most strongly and consistently has sought to put the mark of just war thought on contemporary Christian reasoning about war; in the debate of the 1950s and 1960s this brought him closer to Catholic thought than to the developing pacifism of liberal Protestantism.[25]

Where, then, do we stand today in asking whether the use

of force between nations can be justified? To summarize, international law says that defense is the only just cause, leaving the exact content of the idea of defense to include actions taken in reaction to aggressive uses of force already accomplished. Retaliation is thus allowed, and therefore a second strike (in response to a first) by strategic nuclear missiles is legitimate by this set of rules. The thought of recent popes has generally followed the same lines, though there has been some restriction on the use of force in retaliation, as in the American Catholic bishops' pastoral letter. More restrictive yet is the position of nuclear pacifism, holding that all use of war is immoral in the present age because of the devastation an inevitable escalation to all-out exchange of strategic weapons would wreak.

The Implications of Defense as Just Cause

It is time to take some stock of these various positions. In particular, three issues require to be examined critically: the exact nature of the idea of defense, the question of first use of force versus second use in response, and the question whether retaliation is to be allowed. These are all closely related issues. In answering them we will also reach an implicit conclusion regarding the nuclear pacifist's rejection of the justice of all war today.

The focal problem is that of first use of force. In three major twentieth-century documents of international law, the League of Nations Covenant, the Kellogg-Briand Pact (Pact of Paris), and the United Nations Charter, first resort to force is increasingly strongly rejected. For the concept of defense to be meaningful, it must be defense against something, and in contemporary international law that something has for practical purposes (though there is still some debate on the issue) been defined as first use of force.[26] Defense, then, becomes, by definition, second use. Within the framework of any given conflict, this would seem implicitly to legitimize all three of the traditional concepts of defense, and this is why, in the context of international law, the idea of defense has remained elastic enough to include all three traditional concepts. A military reaction aimed at halting or repulsing an invasion across national frontiers would be a case of legitimate defense against an evil in progress.

But modern war may not involve this sort of invasion. Rather, the aggressor may use the tactic of a hit-and-run raid by commandos who, after they have completed their mission and before a defensive force can be deployed against them, return to their own territory. Or the initial use of force may be by air strike or, in the case of the superpowers, a strategic missile strike. In all these cases, if defense means only the repelling of force while it is in the process of being used, then a predator nation might find it easier to employ a short, sharp attack to wound his enemy, then back off and ask for peace, depending on public opinion against retaliation to inhibit the victim from, in turn, wounding the predator. This appears to be exactly the possibility laid open if the advice is seriously taken that "in this age which boasts of its atomic power, it no longer makes sense to maintain that war is a fit instrument with which to repair the violation of justice."[27] Such reasoning loads the moral dice in favor of the nation that commits the injustice in the first place. Deterrence, a defensive posture resting on the threat of unacceptable retaliation, becomes unthinkable on this posture, because the retaliation could no longer be carried out. (This appears to be, in fact, the logic of the American Catholic bishops' pastoral letter, which while accepting the necessity of keeping a strategic nuclear deterrent force in being nevertheless rejects the possibility of actually using that force as immoral.) But international law has held onto this possibility of retaliation nonetheless, and it should continue to do so. For if aggression need not fear response in kind, the brake on aggressive action represented by the threat of such response disappears, making aggression the more likely.

The judgment against retaliation for an injury already given must rest on a calculation of proportionality, and this calculation must be seriously questioned. Is it in fact true that the devastation of a contemporary war is always the greater evil when compared to an increase in violence owing to a diminishing of deterrent restraints on aggressive powers, an increase in the political domination of peaceful peoples by military predators, and the ability of a totalitarian aggressor to punish dissidence by military force with no fear of a reaction in kind? The assumption made by nuclear pacifists is that war today equates to all-out nuclear holocaust, and it is this equation that leads them to the judgment that war is always worse than peace at whatever cost. This calculation of proportionality begins by setting the costs of war at the probable or certain annihilation of all life on earth; compared to this, any such evil as political domination, even if granted to be genuinely evil, is a much smaller cost to bear.[28]

The history of warfare in the nuclear age, though, as we have noted in an earlier discussion, does not sustain the judgment that war inevitably means nuclear Armageddon. Rather, that history has been one of comparative restraint and the avoidance of conflicts in which the superpowers might directly confront each other militarily. Since 1945 the prevailing face of war has been limited war—war fought in limited areas by means less than those potentially available, even though the goals have often been of an extreme and highly ideologically charged nature. This has been the case even when one of the parties has possessed nuclear weapons. So the judgment that contemporary war implies nuclear holocaust is based not on the history of the nuclear age but on an assessment of what destruction the nuclear weapons known to exist in the world could do if they were all used in a conflict. It is less what it intends to appear to be—a reaction to a realistic depiction of the "fate of the earth" under the threat of contemporary war—than it is a statement of an eschatological—and hence unprovable—faith that disaster looms in our future.

In spite of this weakness in the nuclear pacifist position, it must be stressed that history is not a firm guide to future events. It can support but never guarantee one of the arguments against the nuclear pacifist position: that the threat posed by strategic nuclear weapons is so great that they can never be used. This position is at the core of the reasoning that views nuclear armaments as a stabilizing factor in international relations. By making contemporary war potentially so dangerous, it argues, strategic nuclear arsenals have proven to be a great force for peace.[29]

This argument, however, ignores the fundamental moral issue, which is to have a correlation between the values worth preserving or protecting and the means that are available to use in their protection or preservation. The arguments above set up extremes that are essentially incommensurable with anything else in reality. The task is to suit means to ends, and this means reasoning within the realm of relativities, not extremes; it means thinking of contemporary possibilities not in terms of either a life-annihilating holocaust or the inevitability of peace beneath the so-called nuclear umbrella. Even without use of nuclear weapons, under the umbrella they define, lesser conflicts have taken place and continue to be possible in the present and future. It means, equally, not thinking of all our values as absolutes that may be served only by the most extreme means available to us;[30] for if we begin here, the next step is the catastrophe depicted in the nuclear pacifist position.

The Justifiable Defense of Values

The problem of just warfare in the contemporary age is not the problem of warfare in this age as such; rather, it is the problem of how to avoid what Michael Walzer termed "supreme emergency" situations, in which the only recourse, if the supreme values are to be served, is to go beyond the bounds of moral justification and restraint laid down in our cultural experience. This has implications both for statecraft and for international relations, on the one hand, and for military planning and policy on the other. This is not a book on the former, and I have already said a great deal on the latter, arguing that it is a moral duty to develop means of war that can justifiably be employed to counter threats to values when the only means of protecting or preserving them is through force. To develop such means as replacements for reliance on nuclear weapons is a moral imperative to move the world beyond the present stage in which—here the nuclear pacifists are entirely correct—an all-out strategic nuclear exchange, if it were to come to pass, would be grossly destructive of lives and values throughout this planet. I hasten to add, as I have already argued above, that I believe there are sufficient restraining forces in the world today to prevent such a conflagration from occurring, yet the virtually accidental way in which many military conflicts in the past have begun cautions against complacency regarding the effectiveness of these restraints.

In short, if values are to be defended, there must be justifiable means for defending them; otherwise, we are locked in an unenviable dilemma of either not protecting these values against destruction by others or destroying them ourselves through the use of disproportionate and/or indiscriminate means. For a generation and more the United States has given up conventional weapons and military manpower in trade for nuclear weaponry because the latter were more cost-effective. Perhaps it is now possible at last to begin to reverse this direction, gaining in the process more genuine security for the values we hold dear.

Nonetheless, in treating this subject of the justification or the use of military force, we need to confront the problem that there may arise situations of the sort Walzer has called "supreme emergencies."[31] He applied this term to the argument of the British in favor of counterpopulation strategic bombing of Germany in World War II. As I have analyzed Walzer's discussion of this argument elsewhere,[32] it seems to be a case of temporarily overstepping the bounds of one's moral values in order to protect them from utter loss. (Whether in fact this would have happened is not the issue, because persons must always act on their perceptions of reality.) When the counterpopulation bombing began, it was in part a retaliatory measure, though as we have seen above in chapter 6, it was also a reflection of the factors of "total war" assumptions, available technology, air power doctrine, and rage at the Germans. In the present context, a similar case of retaliation might well involve strategic nuclear weapons. The first thing to say about such a possibility is that, even apart from escalation to all-out exchange, a counterpopulation strike is still a violation of noncombatant immunity. The stress I have laid on the moral necessity of developing flexibility in military forces and doctrines is an attempt to find a way out of responding to the evil of a counterpopulation strike with an equally evil counterpopulation strike in return. I am personally convinced that counterforce strikes, as well as being closer to what is required by the moral tradition of justified warfare, are more effective retaliatory means than terror bombing. But even if this view obtains at the highest levels among political and military defense planners and wartime decision makers, it matters little if the means are not available for such a response. This was the technological issue confronted by the British, quite apart from all the other issues they faced when defending against the Nazi threat. This line of reflection implies development of strategies of retaliation that, while effective, would not involve attacking noncombatants as such and also would restrict collateral damage to noncombatants from strikes at legitimate targets.

In second place on this problem, it is important to accept that circumstances may still arise in which such discrimination is impossible to achieve, so that the only course left, if an effective defense is to be attempted, is that taken by the British in deciding for counterpopulation bombing. This is the sort of case in which high values may, in the best judgment available, be preserved only at the cost of actions which temporarily themselves transgress those very values. Is there anything in just war tradition that would tend to support such action?

The answer, I think, can be found in the argument of a figure frequently mentioned already in this book, the early modern Spanish schoolman Franciscus de Victoria. Victoria was, more than most of his contemporaries and more than the just war tradition before him, especially conscious of the ambiguities in struggles between nations, and as a result he was the first major figure in this developing moral tradition on war to take seriously the idea that, to the most objective observers, a war might appear just on both sides at once.[33] In such cases, he reasoned, both sides should be most scrupulous to observe the restraints given in the *jus in bello* ideas of noncombatant immunity and proportion; otherwise, the party that was in fact (appearances aside) in the wrong would be piling up guilt upon guilt. It does not take a surfeit of realism about international relations, whether in Victoria's time or today, to recognize that most conflicts between states are of such an ambiguous nature; thus a chastened realism about one's own position should serve as a restraint on unlimited military means. But what of the other case, when one knows one's own cause to have justice on its side? Such cases exist as well as the ambiguous ones, Victoria thought; justice here did not mean *absolute* rightness in everything, but rather rightness relative to what the enemy stood for. So also the term *justice* should be understood in our own time, and like Victoria we too should admit that such cases exist. It was Churchill's judgment against Hitler's Gemany that Britain had the just cause; this too was the United States judgment against Japan after the Pearl Harbor attack, quite apart from any other considerations that emerged later of Japanese treatment of prisoners of war or conquered populations. Even though Germany had not directly attacked the United States prior to this country's declaration of war, there should be little doubt, especially in retrospect, that it was just to fight against the Nazis because of the atrocities they performed and the values they sought to promulgate in the world. So let us grant that some cases may arise, in our future as in the past, in which the cause is known to be just and in which the most fundamental human values we hold are threatened. What then?

Victoria treated this possibility in thinking of the siege of a city—perhaps the closest analogue in traditional thought to countercity bombing. In such a case, where the act of siege itself threatens and harms noncombatants within the city, and where the taking of the city through attack during the course of the siege would inevitably also cause death and other destruction to noncombatants as well as to the combatant defenders, Victoria reasoned that it was within the scope of justice to lay siege and attack the city anyway.[34] His point appears to have been the same as Churchill's, though expressed in a context of attack rather than defense: when one is sure of one's own justice and of the enemy's injustice, one may temporarily and in specific cases go beyond the limits, even harming noncombatants. But for Victoria—and for all who would take his precedent as advice—it remained that this was what should be said about a specific kind of case, a case in which not only did the besiegers possess justice but one in which, as Victoria makes clear, *there were no other options available*. Given such options, the limits still applied.

The Relation of the Justice of War to the Means of War: Two Orienting Questions

We may move away from the consideration as raised in the previous section with two questions to be posed to ourselves. First, in any and every armed conflict to which we may be party, is the preponderance of justice clearly on our side and that of injustice clearly upon the enemy's? In thinking about this question the international law criterion of just cause as defense against aggression may serve as a convenient focus, but as we have seen, its own inherent ambiguity means that we must push further into our moral tradition for a satisfactory answer. What is important, from the standpoint of this tradition, is not so much the priority of the use of force as the necessity that compels that justice can be served only through force. (This, I take it, is what is implied in the traditional requirement that force be a last resort after all else has failed.) And what is further important is to avoid the delusions of the sort that Victoria himself rejected when, going contrary to the tradition before him, he declared that to fight a war solely for religion did not satisfy the requirements of justice. In our day, this means that we may not rely upon ideological differences as a surrogate for a genuinely just cause in which to employ force. The second question we should pose to ourselves also comes from the caution employed by Victoria: Is there no other way to gain our just ends without employing force beyond the limits of discrimination and proportionality? If there is, even if the achievement of the ends takes longer and is more costly to us than would be the case if we transgressed these limits, then we are bound to use them. Together these two questions force us to think with utmost seriousness about exceeding just war limits even when our cause is surely a just one, and they impose genuine restraints on the use of extreme measures that, finally, if we follow Victoria, may be used if nothing else avails.

It is perhaps dangerous to end this chapter on such a note, for not everyone may wish to address these questions as scrupulously as Victoria did, or as we must if we would be faithful to our tradition on morality in warfare. But to conclude here is not to open the door to unlimited conduct of war, which this book has everywhere opposed. Rather it is to bring us face-to-face with the hard moral self-searching that we are required to undertake if we would act in ways that go beyond what these traditional limits allow. Since the countercity bombing of World War II there has been a widespread assumption that all-out means are justified in *any* war in which we may find ourselves; the irony of our present historical age is that this assumption is shared by hawks and doves alike, for their own reasons.[35] To take seriously that notion that there may be indeed some occasions when extraordinary means may be used, and to reflect that these may be expected to be rare indeed, may help to move moral debate over contemporary war away from a casual assumption that war cannot and should not be restrained, and toward a recovery of the moral tradition that recognizes just causes and just limits of war.

Notes

Chapter 1. The Utility of Just War Categories

1. CF. Paul Ramsey, *The Just War: Force and Political Responsibility* (New York: Charles Scribner's Sons, 1968), p. 164.

2. For further discussion of this point, see my *Just War Tradition and the Restraint of War* (Princeton: Princeton University Press, 1981), chap. 5; cf. Frederick H. Russell, *The Just War in the Middle Ages* (Cambridge: Cambridge University Press, 1971), passim.

3. *Just War Tradition and the Restraint of War;* see also my *Ideology, Reason, and the Limitation of War* (Princeton: Princeton University Press, 1976), chap. 1.

4 Cf. Augustine, *The City of God* 19.7. See further Paul Ramsey, *War and the Christian Conscience* (Durham: Duke University Press, 1961), chap. 2.

5. Thomas Aquinas, *Summa Theologica* 2/2, quest. 40, art. 1. See further my *Ideology, Reason, and the Limitation of War,* chap. 1.

6. See Robert W. Tucker, *The Just War* (Baltimore: Johns Hopkins University Press, 1960); Ralph B. Potter, *War and Moral Discourse* (Richmond: John Knox Press, 1969), pp. 51–54; and Russell F. Weigley, *The American Way of War* (New York: Macmillan, 1973), chaps. 14–18 passim.

7. For discussion of this development, see my *Ideology, Reason, and the Limitation of War,* chaps. 3 and 4.

8. See further my discussion in "Toward Reconstructing the Jus ad Bellum," *The Monist* 57 (October 1973): 461–88.

9. For fuller discussion of this point, see my *Just War Tradition and the Restraint of War*, chap. 5, and Russell, *The Just War in the Middle Ages*, chap. 4.

10. This, I take it, is the reason why international law requires partisan forces to have a responsible commander if they are to enjoy treatment as legitimate soldiers. Beyond this the principle is recognized in various other ways; cf., for example, Michael Walzer, *Just and Unjust Wars* (New York: Basic Books, 1977), pp. 98–101, and William V. O'Brien, *The Conduct of Just and Limited War* (New York: Praeger, 1981), pp. 158–62.

11. *The Tree of Battles of Honoré Bonet*, trans. and ed. G. W. Coopland (Cambridge: Harvard University Press, 1949), p. 189.

Chapter 2. Can Contemporary Armed Conflicts Be Just?

1. Franciscus de Victoria, *De Indis et De Jure Belli Relectiones*, ed. Ernest Nys, trans. John Pawley R. Bate (Washington: Carnegie Institute, 1917): *De Jure Belli*, secs. 35–37.

2. Walzer, *Just and Unjust Wars*, chap. 16.

3. A recent collection of essays including statements of this position and criticism of it is Thomas A. Shannon, ed., *War or Peace? The Search for New Answers* (Maryknoll, NY: Orbis Books, 1980), esp. chaps. 1, 2, 4, 6, and 10.

4. Victoria, *De Indis*, sec. 3.7.

5. See his discussion in *Just and Unjust Wars*, pp. 259–62.

6. Cf. Stanley Hoffmann's argument in his *Duties Beyond Borders* (Syracuse: Syracuse University Press, 1981), chap. 2. Both here and later in this discussion the point is not simply that lesser evil should always be chosen over greater evil, but rather that force employed in the service of justice should be recognized as a positive good. There may be occasions in which the better moral choice is determined by considerations of lesser and greater evils; such cases arise in war, and I will treat some examples later on. But there are other cases in which good and evil can be discerned, and these should not be collapsed in the calculation of relative evils.

7. See Ramsey, *War and the Christian Conscience* and *The Just War;* and John Courtney Murray, *Morality and Modern War* (New York: Council on Religion and International Affairs, 1959); cf. my *Just War Tradition and the Restraint of War*, pp. 339–57.

8. The problem with such reasoning, its critics note, is that it does not prove the cause–effect connection. The fact that we in the United States have pursued a policy of strategic nuclear deterrence and have not had war does not itself prove that the deterrence has prevented war. Yet despite this criticism of the logic of deterrence, the majority of strategic theorists would appear to agree that the link has been demonstrated historically, if not logically. Cf. Michael Mandelbaum, "International Stability and Nuclear Order," in *Nuclear Weapons and World Politics*, ed. David C. Gompert et al. (New York: McGraw-Hill, 1977), pp. 15–80.

9. See n. 7 above.

10. Bruce Russett, "A Countercombatant Alternative to Nuclear MADness," in *Ethics and Nuclear Strategy?* ed. Harold P. Ford and Francis X. Winters, S.J. (Maryknoll, NY: Orbis Books, 1977), pp. 124–43.

11. See General Sir John Hackett et al., *The Third World War: August 1985* (New York: Berkley Books, 1980).

12. Cf. Hoffmann, *Duties Beyond Borders*, pp. 81–82.

13. Cf. O'Brien, *The Conduct of Just and Limited War*, part II.

14. Cf. ibid., chap. 1; Johnson, *Just War Tradition and the Restraint of War*, chap. 7.

15. The first corresponds to the traditional criterion of right authority, the second to the criterion of just cause.

16. All three ideas can be found in classic Roman practice; more recently and more directly, the first idea was shaped for Western just war tradition by the Augustinian paradigm discussed above in the introduction, while the latter two concepts were restated by scholastic theology. See my *Ideology, Reason, and the Limitation of War*, pp. 26–43.

17. See the discussion of this definition of *intention* in ibid., p. 40.

18. Niccolo Machiavelli, *The Prince*, chap. 21, "How a Prince Must Act in Order to Gain Reputation."

19. A notable exception was the indiscriminate sowing of antipersonnel mines by the Argentine forces, which continue to menace civilians who venture into certain areas.

20. See O'Brien, *The Conduct of Just and Limited War*, chap. 12.

21. Cf. Antoine Henri Baron de Jomini, *The Art of War* (Westport, CT: Greenwood Press, n. d.; reprint of original publication, Philadelphia: J. B. Lippincott and Co., 1862), pp. 26–29; Francis Lieber, *Guerilla Parties* (New York: D. van Nostrand, 1862); Walzer, *Just and Unjust Wars*, chap. 11; Carnegie Endowment for Interna-

tional Peace, *The Law of Armed Conflicts* (New York: Carnegie Endowment for International Peace, 1971).

22. Cf. Lieber, *Guerilla Parties*, pp. 9, 32.

23. See Dietrich Schindler and Jiri Toman, eds., *The Laws of Armed Conflicts* (Leiden: A. W. Sijthoff; Geneva: Henry Dunant Institute, 1973), passim; Geoffrey Best, *Humanity in Warfare* (New York: Columbia University Press, 1980), chaps. 4, 5.

24. Cf. Walzer, *Just and Unjust Wars*, chaps. 9, 10; for further discussion of noncombatant immunity by means of the rule of double effect, see Ramsey, *War and the Christian Conscience*, pp. 256–60 and passim.

25. Walzer, *Just and Unjust Wars*, pp. 198–204. But Walzer concludes (p. 203): "However the political code is specified, terrorism is the deliberate violation of its norms. For ordinary citizens are killed and no defense is offered—none could be offered—in terms of their individual activities."

26. François, Sieur de la Noue, *The Politicke and Militarie Discourses of the Lord de la Noue* (London: T. C. and E. A. by Thomas Orwin, 1587), p. 225.

27. See further my discussion of the rejection of religion as just cause for war in *Ideology, Reason, and the Limitation of War*, pp. 168–71 and 214–19. The context here was holy war, in which religious truth claims sometimes were employed to justify such extreme forms of violence in war as terror campaigns directed against general populations, pillaging and devastation far beyond any reasonable military need, and gratuitous torture of combatant prisoners and noncombatants alike. The need was to find some way to impose restraint on such extreme measures, to root them out of the practice of war. Over the course of the religious wars the answer became increasingly clear: to deny that religious truth claims could provide justification for war and to regard recourse to violence as justified only when its reasons were in principle open to judgment by third parties standing outside the conflict. This was the consensual position reached in just war tradition by the end of the religious wars of the sixteenth and seventeenth centuries, and it is the position that has been maintained subsequently—perhaps most notably in the international law stream of that tradition. The issue is the same whether the ideological truth claims are religious in nature or not: they must not be allowed to appear to legitimate extreme measures of violence.

28. The classic statement of this idea of right authority came from the medieval canonists; see my discussion in *Just War Tradi-*

tion and the Restraint of War, pp. 150–65; on the extension of this idea to the cases of guerilla warfare and terrorism, cf. Walzer, *Just and Unjust Wars*, pp. 184–88.

Chapter 3. Morally Legitimate Defense

1. On the history of nuclear strategy, see Lawrence Freedman, *The Evolution of Nuclear Strategy* (New York: St. Martin's Press, 1983); on the effect of NATO, cf. Lawrence W. Beilenson, *Survival and Peace in the Nuclear Age* (Chicago: Regnery/Gateway, Inc., 1980); Gompert et al., *Nuclear Weapons and World Politics;* Michael Mandelbaum, *The Nuclear Revolution* (Cambridge: Cambridge University Press, 1981), chaps. 3, 6.

2. See chap. 2, n. 8.

3. United States Catholic Conference, "The Challenge of Peace: God's Promise and our Response," *Origins* 13 (May 19, 1983): 14–19. This is the final draft of this pastoral letter as passed by the bishops. The third draft was published in *Origins* 12 (April 14, 1983): 697–727; the second draft in *Origins* 12 (October 28, 1982): 305–28. These bear the same title as the final version.

4. Ramsey, *War and the Christian Conscience*, chaps. 2, 3.

5. See Johnson, *Ideology, Reason, and the Limitation of War* and *Just War Tradition and the Restraint of War.*

6. See my works cited above; cf. Walzer, *Just and Unjust Wars.*

7. Hague Convention IV (1907), sec. 2, chap. 1; in Schindler and Toman, *The Laws of Armed Conflicts*, pp. 76–77.

8. Cf. Best, *Humanity in Warfare*, for a full discussion of the development of the theme of humanity in international law.

9. John Locke, *An Essay Concerning the True Original, Extent and End of Civil Government*, sec. 16, 179–83, 189–92, cf. Johnson, *Ideology, Reason, and the Limitation of War*, pp. 232–40.

10. See, for example, Ramsey, *The Just War*, chap. 15.

11. For a fuller exposition of this theme, see Johnson, *Just War Tradition and the Restraint of War*, chaps. 7, 8, and idem., "The Cruise Missile and the Neutron Bomb: Some Moral Reflections," *Worldview* 20 (December 1977): 20–26.

12. Cf. Mandelbaum, *The Nuclear Revolution*, chap. 1.

13. Ibid.

14. For fuller treatment, see Johnson, *Just War Tradition and the Restraint of War*, chap. 5.

15. For fuller treatment, see ibid., chap. 7.

16. One of the best recent expressions of this view is that of Paul Fussell in *The Great War and Modern Memory* (New York and London: Oxford University Press, 1975).

17. See, for example, the discussion of the position taken by recent popes in Murray, *Morality and Modern War;* see further chapter 8 below.

18. See the chapter by John Garnett in John Baylis, Kenneth Booth, John Garnett, and Phil Williams, *Contemporary Strategy* (New York: Holmes and Meier, 1975), especially pp. 121–24.

19. Victoria, *De Jure Belli*, secs. 36–37. See further the discussion of this point in chapter 8 below.

20. Victoria, *De Jure Belli*, secs. 27–30, 42, 57, 58; *De Indis*, sec. 3.7. See my discussion of this idea in *Ideology, Reason, and the Limitation of War*, pp. 185–95.

21. Cf. Walzer on the idea of "supreme emergency" in *Just and Unjust Wars*, pp. 245, 247–50, 251–55, 261, 267, 268, 274, 323, 327. See further chapter 8 below.

22. Cf. the argument of Paul Ramsey in "A Political Ethics Context for Strategic Thinking," in *Strategic Thinking and Its Moral Implications*, ed. Morton A. Kaplan (Chicago: The University of Chicago Center for Policy Study, 1973), pp. 101–47.

23. Mandelbaum, *The Nuclear Revolution*, chap. 2.

24. Contemporary military thinking on the defense of Europe, in considerable contrast to the political and economic reasoning I have mentioned, stresses the need for lowered reliance on nuclear forces and increased reliance on conventional ones, including high-technology "smart" weapons.

25. Cf., for example, James F. Childress, "Who Shall Live When Not All Can Live?" *Soundings* 53 (Winter 1970): 339–55. The problem of a lottery, in my view, is that it fails to maximize the resources of the society, thus increasing the general burden upon the populace as a whole in the name of an abstractly conceived "equality." There is admittedly a problem with the administration of a "selective service" draft at the margins—that is, in hard cases; yet this is no reason to repudiate the entire concept. If farmers, for example, are more necessary to a legitimate military effort and the overall good of the society than college professors, I see no reason why society as a whole, through legislation, should not give draft exemptions to the former and not to the latter, establish different quotas for each, or find some other way to maximize the general good and minimize the general burden shared by all. See further my discussion of conscientious objection to military service in chapter 7 below.

Chapter 4. Weapons Limits and the Restraint of War

1. For further analysis and justification of these arguments, see my *Ideology, Reason, and the Limitation of War* and *Just War Tradition and the Restraint of War.*

2. See, for example, the essays by Thomas Nagel, R. B. Brandt, and R. M. Hare in *War and Moral Responsibility*, ed. Marshall Cohen et al. (Princeton: Princeton University Press, 1974), pp. 3–61.

3. Thus, for example, when the international lawyers McDougal and Feliciano discuss the law of war, they define it as having to do with the tension between military necessity and the principle of humanity, or, in their phrase combining these opposite notions, "the minimum unnecessary destruction of values." A positive law definition of such values can be found in international law, but aside from such definition these values have no particular content; like the economic principle of utility, *values* here is an empty term waiting to have specific content poured into it. See Myres McDougal and Florentino P. Feliciano, *Law and Minimum World Public Order* (New Haven: Yale University Press, 1961), pp. 82, 522, 528–29.

4. Another way of making this point is that pacifism applies a morality of aspiration to war, while just war tradition instead attempts to provide a morality of duty. Cf. Lon L. Fuller, *The Morality of Law* (New Haven: Yale University Press, 1964), pp. 3–32.

5. The *jus ad bellum*, as noted above, has to do with the right or justice of resorting to war, while the *jus in bello* concerns limits on what it is right to do in war.

6. See Russell, *The Just War in the Middle Ages*, pp. 156ff.

7. See Emmerich de Vattel, *Law of Nations*, sec. 169; cf. secs. 166–68.

8. See Locke, *Essay Concerning Civil Government*, sec. 183; cf. secs. 180–93.

9. Grotius, *The Law of War and Peace*, bk. 2, chap. 4.

10. Cf. the *Postulata* on war presented to Vatican Council I in 1870, citing the "intolerable" costs of military expenditures that cause nations to "groan under the burden" thus imposed; in John Eppstein, *The Catholic Tradition of the Law of Nations* (Washington: Catholic Association for International Peace, 1935), p. 132.

11. For the texts of these agreements, see Schindler and Toman, *The Laws of Armed Conflicts*, pp. 95–149.

12. Cf. John Ulrich Nef, *War and Human Progress* (Cambridge: Harvard University Press, 1952), pp. 24–32.

13. Cf. Russell, *The Just War in the Middle Ages*, pp. 154–59.

14. Francis Lieber, "Remarks on 'incendiary balls' or 'rifle bombs,'" Huntington Library Lieber Collection, no. LI 392; cf. Lieber, *Manual of Political Ethics* 2 vols. (Boston: Charles C. Little and James Brown, 1838, 1839), p. 660: "[I]t is my duty to injure my enemy, as enemy, the most seriously as I can, in order to obtain my end, whether this be protection, or whatever else. The more actively this rule is followed out, the better for humanity, since intense wars are of short duration."

15. The reference is to the St. Petersburg Declaration; see Schindler and Toman, *The Laws of Armed Conflicts*, pp. 95–96.

16. See the discussion of this attitude in my "Just War, the Nixon Doctrine, and the Future Shape of American Military Policy," in *The Year Book of World Affairs 1975* (London: Stevens and Sons, 1975), pp. 139–44.

17. This point is made at more length in the essay just cited. I think also, though, of the rather abrupt switch made by numerous supporters of the American involvement in Vietnam when it became apparent that the United States could not—or would not—"win" it by employing our vastly superior military force. Suddenly these supporters of the war became its opponents; they wanted out every bit as badly as the antiwar faction did. Beyond this example, my larger point is the danger of the politics of extremes compared to the politics of moderation—represented here by the just war tradition.

18. See Ramsey, *War and the Christian Conscience*, passim, and *The Just War*, particularly pp. 430–31.

19. Ramsey, again, has done more to explore this matter than anyone else; see *The Just War*, chaps. 11 and 15.

20. For this argument in extended form, see Mandelbaum, "International Stability and Nuclear Order," especially pp. 31–58.

21. See Schindler and Toman, *The Laws of Armed Conflicts*, pp. 99ff., 107f., 109ff., and 125ff.

22. Ramsey, *The Just War*, chap. 19.

23. Schindler and Toman, *The Laws of Armed Conflicts*, pp. 99ff. and 125ff.

24. The United Nations Resolution of 1961 on the prohibition of use of nuclear and thermonuclear weapons (Schindler and Toman, *The Laws of Armed Conflicts*, pp. 121ff.) has not been generally adopted, and the SALT treaties are actually structured so as to allow particular sorts of loopholes to each signatory.

25. Cf. Francis X. Winters, S.J., "The Nuclear Arms Race: Machine versus Man," chap. 9 in Ford and Winters, *Ethics and Nuclear Strategy?*

26. Michael Mandelbaum, *The Nuclear Question* (Cambridge: Cambridge University Press, 1979), chap. 3. The point is that the new weapons were treated operationally as bigger versions of the old ones. Some strategists from this early period stressed the qualitative differences between nuclear and conventional weapons that implied a new tack in thinking about how to use nuclear arms; cf. Bernard Brodie, *The Absolute Weapon* (New York: Harcourt Brace, 1946). But the results in strategic policy did not manifest such a discontinuity.

27. See n. 20 above.

Chapter 5. Weapons, Tactics, and Morality in War

1. Mandelbaum, *The Nuclear Revolution*, chap. 1. Cf. above, chap. 3, nn. 1, 12, and 23, and chap. 4, n. 26.

2. Fussell, *The Great War and Modern Memory*, esp. pp. 31–32, 175–78, and 310–14; cf. above, chap. 3, n. 16.

3. The theme identified by Fussell is a familiar one in novels and memoirs about the Vietnam War; see, for example, Michael Herr, *Dispatches* (New York: Avon Books, 1978), and Philip Caputo, *A Rumor of War* (New York: Ballantine Books, 1977).

4. For an elaboration of this argument, see O'Brien, *The Conduct of Just and Limited War*, chaps. 9–14.

5. See further Best, *Humanity in Warfare*, for a history of the development of the law of war, the *jus in bello*.

6. The moral requirements of proportionality and discrimination in war imply the use of no more force than is necessary in a specific situation and the avoidance of harm to noncombatants. These are at least the most minimal—and most general—implications of these two moral principles, and the advantage of stating them in this way is that there the closeness to the military principles of economy of force and conservation of available force can be seen most clearly. If moral discussion of war is to mean anything at all in practical terms, then both moral analysts and military persons must recognize that, where the prosecution of war is concerned, both are speaking the same language—though perhaps in different dialects. And, in fact, historically the development of moral guidelines for the conduct of war depended heavily on reflection by military people on the need to apply the force available to them efficiently and with restraint, so that the harm they would do would not outweigh the good and so that military power would not

be squandered to the point of creating weakness. There is, of course, a difference between thinking of noncombatant immunity in terms of the right of the innocent to be left alone and the need to keep soldiers in good discipline, hence apart from rape and pillage of noncombatants; yet in practice the desired results converge. Similarly, the principle of economy of force may aim chiefly at ensuring that a captured strongpoint retains some military useful-ness for the forces that take it, or even more broadly at making certain that force is not expended in such quantities that there is not enough to go around; at the same time the moral principle of proportionality may, as in Augustine, Vattel, or modern humanitar-ian international law, be rooted in a concern for the humanity of the enemy. Yet these two approaches converge also. The fact of common ancestry between the military and moral principles of restraint in war and the further fact that these two sets of princi-ples point toward convergent behavior in the circumstances of war establish the possibility and the potential significance of dialogue across the two "dialects" represented here within just war tradi-tion. This chapter attempts to carry on such a dialogue through examination of the implications of weapons and military tactics for the moral conduct of war.

7. See above, chap. 4, n. 14.

8. For a justification of this position, see Winston Churchill, *The Hinge of Fate* (New York: Bantam Books, 1962), p. 770.

9. See further my discussion of the idea of limited war in his-tory: *Just War Tradition and the Restraint of War*, chap. 7.

10. See further the "American just war doctrine" of the Eisen-hower–Dulles era described by Tucker in his *The Just War.*

11. If discrimination is taken as a moral absolute, then it would not be possible to allow this. But if it is regarded as a grave moral responsibility to be ranged alongside other competing moral re-sponsibilities, then the possibility I have identified as a last resort may prove the best action available. The limited wars of the eigh-teenth century were fought with an implicit distinction between noncombatants in the battle area and others outside it, and this practice in fact defined an alternative understanding of noncomba-tant immunity within developing moral tradition on war. An anal-ogy may perhaps lie in the moral perception of parents who, with one infant child suffering from total kidney failure, decide in favor of a transplant from another of their children, even though the donor is not able to give personal consent and is harmed by the action taken to save the sibling's life.

12. This idea can be traced at least to the time of Joshua, when Israelite soldiers were enjoined from destroying vine and fruit trees, whose sustenance would be needed after the war. See Deuteronomy 20 : 19–20. See further my discussion in "The Meaning of Non-Combatant Immunity in the Just War/Limited War Tradition," *Journal of the American Academy of Religion* 39 (June 1971): 151–70.

Chapter 6. Strategic Targeting

1. Hague Rules of Air Warfare, 1922–23, arts. 22–26; pp. 142–43 in Schindler and Toman, *The Laws of Armed Conflicts*.

2. Johnson, *Just War Tradition and the Restraint of War*, chap. 8.

3. For discussion see A. Russell Buchanan, *The United States and World War II* (New York: Harper and Row, 1964), pp. 187–88, and B. H. Liddell Hart, *History of the Second World War* (New York: Putnam's, 1970), pp. 589–93.

4. Buchanan, *The United States and World War II*, pp. 188, 191; Liddell Hart, *History of the Second World War*, pp. 590–95.

5. Buchanan, *The United States and World War II*, p. 191; Liddell Hart, *History of the Second World War*, pp. 591, 595.

6. Ramsey, *The Just War*, p. 59.

7. Sir Roger Williams, *The Actions of the Lowe Countries* (London: Humfrey Lownes for Matthew Lownes, 1618), p. 88.

8. Cf. Liddell Hart, *History of the Second World War*, pp. 610–12; Walzer, *Just and Unjust Wars*, chap. 16.

9. For a recent discussion of the issue of accuracy, see Thomas Powers, "Choosing a Strategy for World War III," *The Atlantic Monthly* 250 (November 1982): 82–110.

10. Buchanan, *The United States and World War II*, pp. 191–92; Liddell Hart, *History of the Second World War*, pp. 593–95.

11. Powers, "Choosing a Strategy for World War III," p. 88; for discussion of American strategic policy in the period between 1945 and 1960, see Freedman, *The Evolution of Nuclear Strategy*, secs. 1–5, and Mandelbaum, *The Nuclear Question*, chap. 3.

12. See Mandelbaum, "International Stability and Nuclear Order."

13. The corresponding terms generally used in contemporary American military discussion are *countervailing* (for counterforce) and *countervalue* (for counterpopulation) strategy.

14. The former is the scenario for nuclear holocaust generally painted by opponents of nuclear weapons, while the latter sort of scenario finds increasing expression in military plans; witness the limited countercity exchange in a book reflecting NATO analytical thought, Hackett, *The Third World War*, chaps. 25, 26.

15. See above, chap. 5, n. 11.

16. A fourth possible class of targets would need to be included in considering a protracted conflict; manufacturing, support, supply, and transportation facitilies. In a long war the direct aid these would provide to military action would classify them among legitimate combatant targets; in a brief conflict, however, this impact would not determine the outcome in any important way, and it would be superfluous and unnecessary to include them among potential strategic targets for the short term.

17. For a specific case of such argument, see Russett, "A Countercombatant Alternative to Nuclear MADness."

18. Grotius, *The Law of War and Peace*, bk. 3, chap. 11, secs. 4–7; Locke, *Essay Concerning Civil Government*, secs. 179–80.

19. Cf. Walzer, *Just and Unjust Wars*, pp. 197–204.

Chapter 7. Individual Decisions and Morality in War

1. Helmut Thielicke, *Theological Ethics*, vol. 2, *Politics* (Philadelphia: Fortress Press, 1969), pp. 519–38.

2. 401 U.S. 437 (1971).

3. See Johnson, *Ideology, Reason, and the Limitation of War*, pp. 55–59.

4. Ibid., cf. p. 246.

5. The recent pastoral letter of the American Catholic bishops, however, endorses both general and selective conscientious objection; see United States Catholic Conference, "The Challenge of Peace," final version, p. 24.

6. Victoria, *De Indis et De Jure Belli Relectiones*.

7. Karl Barth, *Church Dogmatics*, vol. 3, *The Doctrine of Creation* (Edinburgh: T. & T. Clark, 1961), pt. 4, pp. 450–70.

8. *The Swedish Discipline, Religious, Civile, and Military* (London: John Dawson for Nathaniel Butter and Nicholas Bourne, 1632).

9. Fussell, *The Great War and Modern Memory*, pp. 175–78.

10. See further my discussion of this issue in "Toward Reconstructing the *Jus ad Bellum*."

Chapter 8. The Causes of War and the Restraint of War

1. This particular three-part formulation appears to have entered Western just war consciousness through Maimonides' thought; see the use of Maimonides in Henry Ainsworth's *Annotations upon the Five Books of Moses* (London: John Bellamie, 1627), passim. Most non-Jewish commentators concentrate on the holy war theme in the Old Testament: cf. James A. Aho, *Religious Mythology and the Art of War* (Westport, CT: Greenwood Press, 1981), chap. 9, and Russell, *The Just War in the Middle Ages*, pp. 8–9.

2. For a fuller summary of the Roman idea of just war see Russell, *The Just War in the Middle Ages*, pp. 4–8.

3. See further Johnson, *Ideology, Reason, and the Limitation of War*, chap. 1.

4. Alfred Vanderpol, in his *La Doctrine scholastique du droit de guerre* (Paris: A. Pedone, 1919), p. 250, makes this the centerpiece of premodern just war thought. This is surely going too far; see Johnson, *Ideology, Reason, and the Limitation of War*, pp. 26–33.

5. See further Russell, *The Just War in the Middle Ages*, chaps. 5 and 6; Johnson, *Just War Tradition and the Restraint of War*, pp. 156–61, and *Ideology, Reason, and the Limitation of War*, pp. 53–64.

6. See further Johnson, *Ideology, Reason, and the Limitation of War*, pp. 154–58; cf. pp. 158–71.

7. See Grotius, *The Law of War and Peace*, bk. 2, chaps. 1, 22; cf. Johnson, *Ideology, Reason, and the Limitation of War*, pp. 214–22.

8. This is perhaps the most serious problem in the restraint of war today. See further Johnson, *Ideology, Reason, and the Limitation of War*, pp. 259–74.

9. For discussion of this issue see Johnson, "Toward Reconstructing the *Jus ad Bellum*."

10. Murray, *Morality and Modern War*, p. 9.

11. Pope John XXIII, *Pacem in Terris;* for discussion of the implications of this statement, see Ramsey, *The Just War*, pp. 192–210.

12. Pope Paul VI, *Never Again War!* (New York: United Nations Office of Public Information, 1965), pp. 37–39.

13. United States Catholic Conference, "The Challenge of Peace," final version, p. 15. For the two earlier versions publicly available see above, chapter 3, note 3.

14. Letter of William Clark to the Bishops' Ad Hoc Committee on War and Peace, July 30, 1982, first cited in United States

Catholic Conference, "The Challenge of Peace," second draft, p. 328, n. 40.

15. United States Catholic Conference, "The Challenge of Peace," second draft, pp. 311–12.

16. United States Catholic Conference, "The Challenge of Peace," third draft, pp. 709, 718; final version, pp. 12–13, 21–22.

17. Ibid., final version, p. 11.

18. Ibid.

19. Ibid., pp. 11, 13–14, and passim.

20. Ibid., pp. 13, 21–22, 26.

21. Ibid., pp. 14–19.

22. See, for example, World Council of Churches, Geneva Assembly, "Structures of International Cooperation—Living Together in a Pluralistic World Society," Report of Section III, especially paragraphs 94–95. Some critics of the World Council, while accepting this characterization of its policies as nuclear pacifist, would hold that the support the council has extended to some revolutionary movements shows that it does not entirely or consistently embrace pacifist principles. See, for example, Ernest Lefever, *Amsterdam to Nairobi: The World Council of Churches and the Third World* (Washington, D.C.: Ethics and Public Policy Center, 1979).

23. Ernie Regehr, *Militarism and the World Military Order: A Study Guide for Churches* (Geneva: Commission of the Churches on International Affairs of the World Council of Churches, 1980), p. 65.

24. Evangelical Church in Germany (Evangelische Kirche in Deutschland), *The Preservation, Promotion, and Renewal of Peace*, *EKD Bulletin* Special Issue, October 1981.

25. See Ramsey, *The Just War* and *War and the Christian Conscience*.

26. Cf. Johnson, "Toward Reconstructing the *Jus ad Bellum*," pp. 464–75.

27. See above, n. 11.

28. Theologian Stanley Hauerwas, in "On Surviving Justly: An Ethical Analysis of Nuclear Disarmament," a paper read at the Annual Meeting of the American Academy of Religion, New York, December 20, 1982, takes pains to distinguish this position from genuine pacifism and from Christian ethical motivations, calling it by the name "survivalism." One of the most widely publicized recent statements of this "survivalist" position (also cited by Hauerwas) is Jonathan Schell's *The Fate of the Earth* (New York: Alfred Knopf, 1982).

29. See above, chap. 2, n. 8, and chap. 4, n. 20.

30. I think particularly of the position of John Foster Dulles, who justified massive retaliation strategy by identifying the values of the United States with moral rightness itself; see the critical analysis of this position and its implications in Tucker, *The Just War: A Study in Contemporary American Doctrine.*

31. Walzer, *Just and Unjust Wars,* pp. 251–68.

32. Johnson, *Just War Tradition and the Restraint of War,* pp. 20–30.

33. See Victoria, *De Indis,* sec. 2 and sec. 3. 6–8. For further discussion, see Johnson, *Ideology, Reason, and the Limitation of War,* pp. 185–95.

34. Victoria, *De Jure Belli,* secs. 36–37.

35. For doves the assumption that any (contemporary) war must inevitably be an unlimited war provides support for their argument that all war must be abolished. For hawks the assumption in favor of all-out means gives strength to rhetoric about the possibility of "winning" totally in a military conflict, not having to settle for limited objectives secured by limited military means. In practice the United States has not been guided by this assumption in the military conflicts in which it has been involved since World War II—most importantly those in Korea and Vietnam. Doves typically ignore the historical lessons taught by these (and other) cases of limited contemporary war, while hawks pounce on the incomplete and undesirable results of these conflicts as signs that future wars should be fought with all-out military means.

Select Bibliography

Aho, James A. *Religious Mythology and the Art of War*. Westport, CT: Greenwood Press, 1981.

Ainsworth, Henry. *Annotations upon the Five Books of Moses*. London: John Bellamie, 1627.

Aquinas, Thomas, St. *Summa Theologica*. 3 vols. London: R. & T. Washbourne; New York: Benziger Brothers, 1912–22.

Augustine, St. *Basic Writings of St. Augustine*. 2 vols. Edited, with introduction and notes, by Whitney J. Oates. New York: Random House, 1948.

Barth, Karl. *Church Dogmatics*, vol. 3, *The Doctrine of Creation*, part 4. Edinburgh: T. & T. Clark, 1961.

Baylis, John, Ken Booth, John Garnett, and Phil Williams. *Contemporary Strategy*, New York: Holmes and Meier Publishers, 1975.

Bellenson, Lawrence W. *Survival and Peace in the Nuclear Age*. Chicago: Regnery/Gateway, Inc., 1980.

Best, Geoffrey. *Humanity in Warfare*. New York: Columbia University Press, 1980.

Bonet, Honoré. *The Tree of Battles of Honoré Bonet*. Translated and edited by C. W. Coopland. Cambridge: Harvard University Press, 1949.

Brodie, Bernard. *The Absolute Weapon*. New York: Harcourt Brace, 1946.

Buchanan, A. Russell. *The United States and World War II*. New York, Evanston and London: Harper and Row, 1964.

Caputo, Philip. *A Rumor of War.* New York: Ballantine Books, 1977.

Childress, James F. *Moral Responsibility in Conflicts.* Baton Rouge and London: Louisiana State University Press, 1982.

———. "Who Shall Live When Not All Can Live?" *Soundings* 53 (Winter 1970): 339–55.

Churchill, Winston. *The Hinge of Fate.* New York: Bantam Books, 1962.

Cohen, Marshall, et al., eds. *War and Moral Responsibility.* Princeton: Princeton University Press, 1974.

Eppstein, John. *The Catholic Tradition of the Law of Nations.* Washington: Catholic Association for International Peace, 1935.

Evangelical Church in Germany (*Evangelische Kirche in Deutschland*). *The Preservation, Promotion, and Renewal of Peace. EKD Bulletin* Special Issue, October 1981.

Ford, Harold P., and Francis X. Winters, S.J., eds. *Ethics and Nuclear Strategy?* Maryknoll, NY: Orbis Books, 1977.

Freedman, Lawrence. *The Evolution of Nuclear Strategy.* New York: St. Martin's Press, 1983.

Fuller, Lon L. *The Morality of Law.* New Haven: Yale University Press, 1964.

Fussell, Paul. *The Great War and Modern Memory.* New York and London: Oxford University Press, 1975.

Gompert, David C., et al., *Nuclear Weapons and World Politics.* New York: McGraw-Hill, 1977.

Grotius, Hugo. *De Jure Belli ac Pacis Libri Tres.* Volume 2, translation of the 1646 edition by Francis W. Kelsey et al. Introduction by James Brown Scott. *Classics of International Law.* Oxford: Clarendon Press; London: Humphrey Milford, 1925.

Hackett, General Sir John, et al. *The Third World War: August 1985.* New York: Berkley Books, 1980.

Hauerwas, Stanley. "On Surviving Justly: An Ethical Analysis of Nuclear Disarmament." Paper read at the Annual Meeting of the American Academy of Religion, New York, December 20, 1982.

Herr, Michael. *Dispatches.* New York: Avon Books, 1978.

Hoffman, Stanley. *Duties Beyond Borders.* Syracuse: Syracuse University Press, 1981.

Johnson, James Turner. *Ideology, Reason, and the Limitation of War: Religious and Secular Concepts, 1200–1740.* Princeton and London: Princeton University Press, 1975.

———. "Just War, the Nixon Doctrine, and the Future Shape of American Military Policy." *Year Book of World Affairs 1975.* London: Stevens & Sons Ltd., 1975.

―――. *Just War Tradition and the Restraint of War: A Moral and Historical Inquiry.* Princeton: Princeton University Press, 1981.

―――. "Toward Reconstructing the *Jus ad Bellum.*" *The Monist* 57 (October 1973): 461–88.

Jomini, Antoine Henri Baron de. *The Art of War.* Translated by Capt. G. H. Mendell and Lieut. W. P. Craighill. Westport, CT: Greenwood Press, n. d. Reprint of original publication, Philadelphia: J. B. Lippincott and Co., 1862.

Kaplan, Morton A., ed. *Strategic Thinking and Its Moral Implications.* Chicago: The University of Chicago Center for Policy Study, 1973.

La Noue, François, Sieur de. *The Politicke and Militarie Discourses of the Lord de la Noue.* Translated by E. A. London: T. C. and E. A. by Thomas Orwin, 1587.

Lefever, Ernest. *Amsterdam to Nairobi: The World Council of Churches and the Third World.* Washington: Ethics and Public Policy Center, 1979.

Liddell Hart, B. H. *History of the Second World War.* New York: G. P. Putnam's Sons, 1970.

Lieber, Francis. *Guerilla Parties, Considered with Reference to the Laws and Usages of War.* New York: D. van Nostrand, 1862.

―――. *Instructions for the Government of Armies of the United States in the Field.* U.S. War Department, General Orders No. 100 (1863). New York: D. van Nostrand, 1863.

―――. *Manual of Political Ethics.* 2 volumes. Boston: Charles C. Little and James Brown, 1839.

―――. "Remarks on 'incendiary balls' or 'rifle bombs.' " Huntington Library Lieber Collection, no. LI 392.

Locke, John. *Two Treatises of Civil Government.* London: J. M. Dent and Sons; New York: E. P. Dutton and Co., 1924.

Machiavelli, Niccolo. *The Prince and Discourses.* New York: Modern Library, 1950.

Mandelbaum, Michael. *The Nuclear Question.* Cambridge: Cambridge University Press, 1979.

―――. *The Nuclear Revolution.* Cambridge: Cambridge University Press, 1981.

McDougal, Myres S., and Florentino P. Feliciano. *Law and Minimum World Public Order.* New Haven: Yale University Press, 1961.

Murray, John Courtney. *Morality and Modern War.* New York: Council on Religion and International Affairs, 1959.

Nef, John Ulrich. *War and Human Progress.* Cambridge: Harvard University Press, 1950.

O'Brien, William V. *The Conduct of Just and Limited War.* New York: Praeger Publishers, 1981.
Paul VI, Pope. *Never Again War!* New York: United Nations Office of Public Information, 1965.
Potter, Ralph B. *War and Moral Discourse.* Richmond: John Knox Press, 1969.
Powers, Thomas. "Choosing a Strategy for World War III." *The Atlantic Monthly* 250 (November 1982): 82–110.
Ramsey, Paul. *The Just War: Force and Political Responsibility.* New York: Charles Scribner's Sons, 1968.
———. *War and the Christian Conscience: How Shall Modern War Be Conducted Justly?* Durham: Duke University Press, 1961.
Regehr, Ernie. *Militarism and the World Military Order: A Study Guide for Churches.* Geneva: Commission of the Churches on International Affairs of the World Council of Churches, 1980.
Russell, Frederick H. *The Just War in the Middle Ages.* Cambridge: Cambridge University Press, 1975.
Schell, Jonathan. *The Fate of the Earth.* New York: Alfred Knopf, 1982.
Schindler, Dietrich, and Jiri Toman, eds. *The Laws of Armed Conflicts: A Collection of Conventions, Resolutions, and Other Documents.* Leiden: A. W. Sijthoff; Geneva: Henry Dunant Institute, 1973.
Shannon, Thomas, ed. *War or Peace? The Search for New Answers.* Maryknoll, NY: Orbis Books, 1980.
The Swedish Discipline, Religious, Civile and Military. London: John Dawson for Nathaniel Butter and Nicholas Bourne, 1632.
Thielicke, Helmut. *Theological Ethics.* Volume 2, *Politics.* Philadelphia: Fortress Press, 1969.
Tucker, Robert W. *The Just War: A Study in Contemporary American Doctrine.* Baltimore: Johns Hopkins University Press, 1960.
United States Catholic Conference. "The Challenge of Peace: God's Promise and Our Response." Final version, *Origins* 13 (May 19, 1983): 1–32; third draft, *Origins* 12 (April 14, 1983): 697–727; second draft, *Origins* 12 (October 28, 1982): 305–28.
Vanderpol, Alfred. *La Doctrine scholastique du droit de guerre.* Paris: A. Pedone, 1919.
Vattel, Emmerich de. *The Law of Nations; or Principles of the Law of Nature: Applied to the Conduct and Affairs of Nations and Sovereigns.* Translated from the French. London: n. n., 1740.
Victoria, Franciscus de. *De Indis et De Jure Belli Relectiones.* Translated by John Pawley R. Bate. *Classics of International Law.* Edited by Ernest Nys. Washington: Carnegie Institute, 1917.

Walzer, Michael. *Just and Unjust Wars: A Moral Argument with Historical Illustrations*. New York: Basic Books, 1977.

Weigley, Russell F. *The American Way of War*. New York: Macmillan Publishing Co., Inc.; London: Collier Macmillan Publishers, 1973.

Williams, Sir Roger. *The Actions of the Lowe Countries*. London: Humfrey Lownes for Matthew Lownes, 1618.

Index